KUEI, MY FRIEND

ALSO BY DENI ELLIS BÉCHARD

Vandal Love
Cures for Hunger: A Memoir
The Last Bonobo: A Journey to the Congo
Into the Sun
*White**

* To be published by Talonbooks

ALSO BY NATASHA KANAPÉ FONTAINE

Do Not Enter My Soul in Your Shoes†
Assi Manifesto†
Blueberries and Apricots† (forthcoming)

† Translated by Howard Scott

KUEI, MY FRIEND

A CONVERSATION ON
RACISM AND RECONCILIATION

DENI ELLIS BÉCHARD

AND

NATASHA KANAPÉ FONTAINE

TRANSLATED BY DENI ELLIS BÉCHARD
AND HOWARD SCOTT

TALONBOOKS

Talonbooks
278 East First Avenue, Vancouver, British Columbia, Canada V5T 1A6
www.talonbooks.com

First printing: 2018

Typeset in Caslon
Printed and bound in Canada on 100% post-consumer recycled paper

Interior and cover design by Typesmith
Cover illustration by Chloë Filson

Talonbooks acknowledges the financial support of the Canada Council for the Arts, the Government of Canada through the Canada Book Fund, and the Province of British Columbia through the British Columbia Arts Council and the Book Publishing Tax Credit.

LIBRARY AND ARCHIVES CANADA CATALOGUING IN PUBLICATION

Béchard, Deni Ellis, 1974–
[Kuei, je te salue. English]
     Kuei, my friend : a conversation on racism and reconciliation / Deni Ellis Béchard and Natasha Kanapé Fontaine ; translated by Howard Scott.

Translation of: Kuei, je te salue : conversation sur le racisme.
ISBN 978-1-77201-195-1 (SOFTCOVER)

     1. Béchard, Deni Ellis, 1974– – Correspondence. 2. Kanapé Fontaine, Natasha, 1991– – Correspondence. 3. Indians, Treatment of Canada. 4. Whites – Relations with Indians. 5. Racism – North America. 1. Kanapé Fontaine, Natasha, 1991–, author 11. Title. 111. Title: Kuei, je te salue. English

E78.C2B38513 2018   305.897'071   C2018-900736-2

These letters were written in the fall of 2015.
They are dedicated to all the Indigenous women
and girls who have gone missing and been
murdered in the last thirty years or more,
to the resilient Indigenous women of Val-d'Or,
to the survivors of the Canadian Indian residential schools,
who are stronger than time and dispossession,
as well as to future generations,
so that the words can be spoken
and open up a way toward dialogue
between First Nations and Québécois,
and between all the other peoples who need it.

There is a natural prejudice that leads one to scorn a person who has been his or her inferior long after that person has become his equal. The real inequality resulting from fortune or law is always replaced by an imaginary inequality rooted in mores. [...] After the Moderns abolish slavery, they must still destroy three prejudices that are far more intangible and tenacious: the prejudice of the master, the prejudice of race, and the prejudice of the white man.

—ALEXIS DE TOCQUEVILLE
On Democracy in America (1835)

The racism of a gaze is the most treacherous there is. It does not speak, it does not hit, it does not make audible insults. It is there and its recipient can make no mistake about it. It is a sensation no person who has not been a victim of discrimination can recognize, because it is not part of their experience of the world. [...] You can never say, "Sir or madam, your gaze is an intrusion." There is no reliable code on the subject. It is a question of skin, if I may say so. The gaze of a racist grabs you by the guts.

—JEAN-CLAUDE CHARLES
Manhattan Blues (1985)

By its very nature, racism only permits the victimized race to engage that hatred among its own. Lateral violence among Native people is about our anticolonial rage working itself out in an expression of hate for one another.

—LEE MARACLE
I Am Woman: A Native Perspective on Sociology and Feminism (1996)

CONTENTS

Kuei, My Friend
    Introduction to the English Edition   p. 1

Appendices
    1. Chronology of Events   p. 147

    2. A Few Words in Innu-aimun   p. 152

    3. Questions for Young People
        Exercise 1   p. 154
        Discussion in the classroom on the topic of racism
        Exercise 2   p. 159
        Letter exchange projects between students from different
        communities and cultures
        Exercise 3   p. 161
        Other projects to be done as a group

Acknowledgments   p. 163

INTRODUCTION TO
THE ENGLISH EDITION

This book is an experiment: an agreement to write to each other as openly and as honestly as possible about racism. Our goal was the dialogue and the growth that would result from it, as well as the creation of a template that could help guide and inspire students as they engaged in their own dialogues.

In composing these letters, we knew that our words would be painful, and that we would have to allow ourselves the space to explore and test ideas though writing. Each letter influenced the one that followed, and the process of exchanging ideas, memories, and interpretations continuously shifted our path. The result was a fluid conversation that could have continued indefinitely, and in many ways, it has – in our friendship as well as in our individual work. At no point do we claim to have the best or deepest understanding of racism or of the complex and varied issues concerning race; rather, by writing out our ideas, we were trying to see racism from different points of view and to expand our own understanding of it.

We began this project with the goal of creating a book, and with the support of a publisher, so though we were writing to each other, we were also aware that we would be speaking to our readers. Looking back on the letters, we can see how this affected the tone, since even as we make sense of ideas for ourselves to enlarge our understanding of racism, we are sharing those ideas with our readers in a way that might be more explanatory than if we were merely writing to each other. Our initial audiences for the book were high school- and college-aged, though our readership has turned out to be much larger and in no way limited by age. We have been surprised by how far the book has travelled since its release and how many people have wanted to join us in thinking of ways to heal the divisions and traumas that racism has created in our society.

The conversation around racism varies dramatically throughout North America, and while people in English Canada and the United States have been exploring the subject for longer, the discussion around race remains relatively young in Quebec. Furthermore, Quebec's history and social dynamics have led to distinct manifestations of racism, and we have included footnotes to explain details that might not be immediately evident to English Canadian and American readers. The historical proximity between the Indigenous and Québécois Peoples creates a slightly different context than in many other parts of Canada or the United States. Furthermore, tensions between French and English Canadians present a unique challenge to discussions of racism. The Québécois, while being a colonizing force in their own right, were also a conquered people who were, in turn, colonized and, in many ways, oppressed. This has allowed us to address how layered and complicated prejudice, discrimination, and racism can be – how an oppressed people can oppress another, less powerful group. We also expand the conversation to racism elsewhere, looking at the racism in the United States, the Democratic Republic of the Congo, and Europe. By doing so, we have tried to think about racism as broadly as possible.

Though discussing race requires a certain level of sensitivity and caution, fear often so thoroughly dominates the public discussion that the result can be a stiff politeness and an avoidance of engaging rather than any genuine understanding. Through honesty and patience, we have tried to explore the subject with the intention of learning rather than of being right. The process was deeply uncomfortable for both of us. Simply rereading some of the letters can be painful. And yet, in the two years since the book's publication in French, we have received letters from readers who have wanted to engage in the conversation or who are doing their own exchanges. As envisioned, a number of schools and universities have used the book as a template and have shared those letters with us. We hope that deeper and more nuanced explorations will emerge from this one and ultimately render it obsolete. And in the meantime, we are humbly sharing it in English for those who might find inspiration in the discussion, new paths for their own work, tools for communication, teaching, and activism, or simply ideas worth considering in their daily lives.

Deni Ellis Béchard
Natasha Kanapé Fontaine

1

Kuei Natasha,

As I say hello in your language, I feel the distance separating Indigenous and non-Indigenous Peoples. Over the years, I have learned to greet people in Spanish, Italian, Romanian, German, Farsi, Arabic, Hindi, Japanese, Mandarin, Lingala, and Swahili – even in Classical Latin – but not in a single language of the peoples who have lived in North America for millennia.

This is a symptom of a problem that White people struggle to address.[1] We enjoy vacations in Latin America

---

1   In the French edition, we refer to Indigenous Peoples as *Autochtones* (corresponding to the rarer English words *autochthon* and *autochthonous*) and settlers and foreign transplants, including recent immigrants, as *Allochtones* (English *allochthon* and *allochthonous*). In English, an *autochthon* can refer to an Indigenous or Aboriginal person, whereas *allochthon* has yet to be used for people who come from elsewhere. *Allochthonous* generally refers to geological phenomena, with occasional biological uses. In Indigenous communities in Canada, the term *settler* is increasingly used to refer to allochthons. In this book, we use the terms *settler*, *non-Indigenous*, and *White* in reference to allochthonous North Americans. We recognize that all of these terms can be problematic, in the sense that, like many racial constructions, they are artificial regroupings of diverse people – in the case not only of allochthones but also of autochthones. However, a regrouping such as "White" does represent the many communities of people in North America who primarily identify in this way and benefit from being perceived as such. Newcomers of European descent who arrive on the continent often find themselves included in this identity, whose interests and privileges strongly contrast with those of North America's original inhabitants, who themselves are increasingly allied to protect their interests.

and discussions of multiculturalism, but we generally remain ignorant of Indigenous Peoples. In fact, the reality of their lives often frightens us. By building a wall of ignorance between our communities, we've brought an immense fear into the world. The more we are afraid, the less we know each other, and the fear grows like a cancer. We have become so obsessed with the sickness that we think only of our own well-being and forget the source of the problem.

This is why I am writing to you. We became friends in Sept-Îles, Quebec, last spring, during the North Shore Book Fair, held in the region where you were born. You had returned there to confront a popular Québécois writer who, in a blog for *Le Journal de Montréal*, described Indigenous culture(s) as "deadly" and "antiscientific."

You simply wanted to read her a letter that expressed your point of view: to tell her how hurtful her words were and how much they perpetuated the false and racist image against which your people have fought for centuries. But when you tried to speak, she cut you off and used a microphone so that she could speak over you.

I thought to myself that she should have offered you the microphone, even if she didn't agree with your ideas – especially, it seemed to me, in a space like a book fair that existed for the purpose of intellectual exchange. Rather, she read you the definition of an "Amerindian" that she herself had written in one of her own books. The irony and arrogance of this stunned me. You were there with other Indigenous women, and she could have taken the occasion to have a dialogue with you and to learn directly from the source, but she chose to speak in your place. At that moment, I understood something. We, the non-Indigenous North Americans, have a cultural conviction that we are always right, that our domination over the world indicates that our way of thinking is correct and our actions righteous. That belief is encoded in our culture, rooted in our unconsciousness. We don't know how to listen. We condemn to silence all those who are different from us, and we speak in their place while acting as if we are listening.

I am writing this letter to open a dialogue, not with the goal of placing blame on White people for our racist culture, but rather responsibility. No one of us invented it. We inherited it. Nevertheless, we are responsible for understanding how to change it and then doing so. Of course, this isn't easy, since we struggle even to perceive a way of being that seems so normal to us. We live in our culture the way we breathe the air around us; we take it for granted.

Perhaps it is easier for you to perceive this reality, you who have lived both inside and outside of settler cultures. So, in writing to you, I have two goals: that the letters that we will write over the course of this epistolary exchange form a book of honesty as well as a book of questions. In order to understand the problem, we have to tell our stories, and these will at times hurt both of us, since racism affects those who live on both sides of the division it creates. When we deny the complex humanity of another person, we limit the growth of our humanity: our intelligence, our compassion, and all the qualities that make us human. In this way, when we reduce another person to an idea or a series of prejudices, we reduce our capacity to fully experience our own humanity. Those who see others as caricatures become caricatures themselves.

Above all, I have realized the importance of listening. White people have to learn to share the space for dialogue and find a balance between their words and those of other peoples. I will have many questions to ask you. But to start, I would like to know how you experienced what happened at the book fair where we met.

And also, how do you say "Talk to you soon" in the Innu language?

Deni

2

Kuei, kuei, my friend,

When I wrote these words to begin my very first letter,
my reflex was to ask myself why I'd chosen to say "kuei"
instead of "hello."

It was precisely to go further into this kind of questioning
that we agreed to come together in front of our computer
screens, after the experience we shared at the North Shore
Book Fair in Sept-Îles, Quebec. To write about the relationships between our peoples. Just as much as you've shown an
interest in asking questions about my perceptions, I have
an interest in giving you answers, in exchanging with you
and learning to distinguish between the real and the false
so that we can, perhaps, heal our collective unconscious.
I'd like to learn from you, too.

Do you remember that April 27? I'll tell you, since
you don't know the whole story. I recounted it to you too
quickly that day, I was so upset. I'd seen the indignation
spread through my Indigenous social networks. When that
speaker published that horrible column in the pages of that
newspaper – the most widely read newspaper in Quebec,
both in the Québécois and Indigenous communities –
I was sad to see the kind of slander that someone would
still dare to serve up to the citizens of Quebec. According
to my values and my principles, no doubt coming from
my traditional culture, I couldn't believe someone could

spread such notions to their contemporaries, to people of their community. That was racism. I again felt wounded by so much ignorance. It's what convinced me to co-sign an open letter written by friends from the Indigenous *and* Indigenous-friendly cultural community. And, well, it was exactly for that reason, because of that indignation shared with the vast majority of my friends and their friends and families, in more or less remote communities in Mauricie, on the North Shore, in Gaspésie, that I wanted to give a voice to those who didn't have the ability to speak in public or, simply, couldn't speak French well. Because, sometimes, in this society, being part of a visible minority means not knowing how to speak the dominant language ...

My people had just been publicly smeared. In 2015, I couldn't let that kind of disgusting talk pass without responding. I'll talk to you later about this "survival instinct" that energizes me sometimes. In those moments, I often see an image of a white she-wolf defending her pack.

So I decided to go to the North Shore Book Fair the following weekend. I formulated a public statement to make in front of that woman in order to prove the exact opposite of what she had just said about my people: its supposed inertia. I found motivation by telling myself that my people would see that it was possible to stand up and speak publicly to defend us. In other words, I was using my "open" speech to set an example. Through strict adherence to non-violence, first and foremost, and, above all, through dignity and humanity.

Innu women were there to support me, with all their pride as women, first of all, then as Innu. At the moment when I walked toward the speaker, they all stood up, as agreed. What a sensation! I felt like I was centuries in the past, standing with the women of my nation; being many, but at that same time being one. In spite of our action being perfectly legitimate, we were treated with condescension by that speaker. I'd been warned, so I should have anticipated it. But then I came face to face with the abyss of human ignorance and arrogance.

No one actually needs to be punished for this racist culture. We should instead serve the community good food for the spirit. I am constantly telling Québécois and other peoples who descend from colonizers that it is not their fault. The fault lies with those who created this country on a foundation of racism and discrimination, and the government leaders who have perpetuated this system. That's a proven fact. We, the Indigenous Peoples, have known this from the beginning. We had seen it in our oracles and our camp fires at night, long before the arrival of the "White man" on the continent.

It sounds strange, I know, but just look up the Seven Fires Prophecy on the Internet. It is said to have been revealed to the Anishinaabe people by spiritual entities, about seven generations ago. It predicted that other human beings with pale skins would come by the sea and that we would see animals with horns increase in number (cattle), metal snakes crossing the country (railways and pipelines), and a great spider spinning its web across the entire Earth (the Internet). It declared that if all these predictions came to pass, then the pale people would have vanquished all the land of Turtle Island (the traditional name for the North American continent). The prophecy also said that the seventh generation after the one that received the Seven Fires would rise up to awaken the hearts and minds of those First Nations that have experienced oppression. At that moment, human beings would be faced with a choice: either continue on the path of unlimited growth, materialism, exploitation of human and natural resources, or else take the path of spirituality (because all humans have spirits), rediscover their original relationship with nature, and once again honour the women of their clans in order to perpetuate traditions, peoples, and humanity itself. The great awakening.

But, even though we were warned, there was nothing we could do. And that's where we stand, Deni. So sometimes I wonder about fate. Maybe that's part of another legend, another prophecy.

Our contemporaries need honesty. You and I write, we have the power of writing and speech. Let's make use of it. Let's use it for the right cause: the humanity of our fellow beings. Of our peoples that can't go on not talking to each other, not knowing how to talk to each other.

I, too, will learn. I've been speaking loud and clear for so long that maybe I've already forgotten how to listen. But I will listen. We are less and less afraid. For so long, we have been persecuted and have focused on our pain and, in spite of our fear of being once again betrayed or insulted, we now have to listen. I will listen. Speak to me. Let's talk.

Among us, we commonly say "niaut" for "goodbye." In Mani-utenam and beyond, continuing north on the Quebec Route 138, you mostly hear "iame." And to say "See you soon," in the sense "We will see each other soon," we say "Iame uenapissish," which I translate literally as "Goodbye, for a little time."

Iame uenapissish nuitsheuakan,
Natasha

3

Kuei, kuei, once again,

Today I have been thinking a lot about fear and silence, and it seems to me that the two are inextricably linked, at least in the case of racism. Racism is built on the silence of those whom we reject and of whom we are afraid. When two groups of people dispute questions of power, territory, and resources – as we see in many countries – the space in which they can express their humanity diminishes. Their prejudices prevent them from seeing their fundamental similarities: the ways we must work to create a place for ourselves in the world, how we love, how we grieve ... In short, all of the pleasures and pains of life.[2]

Once we have understood how much we share, the

---

2 In rereading the translation of this letter, I am struck by the infuriating absurdity of having to argue for the basic humanity of any person or group of people, and yet in many of my conversations with people who express racist views, it is, first and foremost, the humanity of the other people that they are denying. During a trip to Scotland, I hitchhiked around the Isle of Skye and was picked up by a Scottish woman who told me that she had walked the Camino de Santiago de Compostela, a pilgrimage in Spain to the shrine where the remains of Saint James are believed to be interred. She said that she met a group of Canadians on the trip and that they often expressed their hatred of Indigenous people, characterizing them as drunks who have alcoholism "in their blood" and aren't capable of participating in society. Before that conversation, I had been thinking about our letters and wondering whether it had really been necessary to argue in favour of people's humanity, given that it should be obvious. But centuries-old ingrained racist ideas and the parochialism of many people in settler cultures oblige us to address this topic.

differences seem insignificant; and nonetheless, it is on the basis of these differences that we build our racist prejudices. There is a great beauty in difference, a beauty that I appreciate more with time, a great diversity of ways of thinking and being on earth. These perspectives nourish our creativity and inspire in us new solutions to resolve our problems.

However, in terms of the great questions that we pose about our existence, we want to believe that we are right, that our ethnic or social group, among the millions that exist on earth, has found the only good way to live. This is arrogance as well as ignorance of history. We persist in insisting to the world that we are right before we have even listened to other points of view or tried other ways of living.

And so, the silence: many aspects of our culture reduce those who differ from the majority to silence. The media has a tendency to show us above all what is negative among others and that incites us to perceive them as a group rather than as individuals. If a White person commits a robbery, I don't spontaneously say, "Whites are all like that. They're all robbers!" But when a person belonging to a marginalized group steals, we react immediately by saying, "They're all like that. They're all thieves!" We erase the wealth of their individuality.

The problem is that the voice of a group is in fact the voice of all of the individuals that constitute it, and if we refuse to accept that a group is composed of a diversity of individuals, we deny the possibility of entering into communication with them. It's for this reason that the article in *Le Journal de Montréal* shocked me. The writer didn't speak of individuals. She made an exaggerated generalization about Indigenous people and their values despite their diversity and complexity. She could have written about the actions of several individuals in particular or about a law that she opposed, and then explained her point of view. She could also have asked questions to Indigenous people who were far more informed than she was. Instead, her article reduced Indigenous people to a caricature and reinforced racist stereotypes, since racism is always based on simplification. For Indigenous people who are trying to be heard and who struggle daily against stereotypes and prejudices, the article was another sign of closure on the part of White people. And for the racists reading the paper – those who feel justified in their negative perceptions of Indigenous Peoples – the article simply confirmed their beliefs without adding any new information or perspectives. I don't expect everyone to be in agreement, only that we accept to listen to different voices without recourse to reductive generalizations.

It's for this reason that we are writing, Natasha: to break the barrier of silence. Maybe *silence* isn't the perfect word, since it's more the voices of one people that are overwhelming and smothering that of the other. White people hear above all their own words, just as the writer at the Book Fair – Denise Bombardier – took her own book to read you the definition of an "Amerindian." Surely it was reassuring for her to hear what she already thought and she felt comforted by the repetition of her ideas. Entering into a dialogue would have been far more difficult and vulnerable. Opening oneself to other points of view is often destabilizing and, to do it well, it is necessary to have humility and respect for those who have a different history and who don't see the world as we do.

So, Natasha, of what are you and your people distrustful? In your experience, how do many Indigenous people perceive Whites? Are they afraid? And, if so, how do they experience that fear and silence?

Iame uenapissish,
Deni

P.S. What does *nuitsheuakan* mean?

15

4

My dear Deni,

Nuitsheuakan means "my friend."

In our communities, it goes without saying that we're happy to see each other. There is no other way to be. To be Innu. I don't know how to explain it. Maybe we want to avoid negative energies. When we're happy, we speak loudly, we laugh hard, and we laugh all the time. When we're sad, we're silent. We don't talk. We are totally wrapped up in our feelings. I believe that our ancestors worked on themselves for a long time, generation after generation, to leave us the legacy of a calm, cheerful disposition. As I told you, in my way of thinking, silence comes with wounds. And wounds generate fear in some cases, especially when the relationship with the other is mixed up with violence rooted in history. Fear is deeply ingrained in human beings: fear of the other, fear of boredom, fear of loneliness, fear of dying, sometimes fear of living ... In the case of racism, I always wonder if an inferiority complex, hidden under a superior attitude, is really the source. Or else envy. Because, in what I've seen so far, everything is masked by pride. Often I think – I don't know why – about passages from the Bible. Lucifer who rebelled out of pride. Isn't that the history of the beginning of the world, as many people have learned it? Of course, those were parables that, like tales, are used to transmit teaching about human beings. For a long time, it's been said that the greatest struggle of the world (or of humans) is the fight against pride, because the foundation of the universe is love. Love for everything that exists. Maybe I'm getting away from the subject, but that's what comes to mind when I try to explain fear of the other. Shrouded by prejudices and ignorance, fear causes us to reject the possibility of acquiring better knowledge and prevents us from thinking about things rationally. It is how relationships between peoples become relationships poisoned by pride on either side.

We're never very far from each other. The territory of Quebec illustrates this idea very well. The First Nations reserves are never very far from Quebec towns and villages. Sometimes, they're separated by just a few kilometres. And often the Whites have gone there, close to Indigenous people, for industrial needs (lumber, iron, petroleum). A forced sharing of territory ... These days communication is sometimes easy. But often it's just the opposite. And everything between the two extremes. In those regions, the members of the two communities are often wounded by mutual ignorance. Each group is part of the imaginary of their neighbours, but, on both sides, no one really sees any further than the end of their nose. We just need to find a way to transform the images that we have of other people, to form our own ideas through direct human contact. Why not open up to each other? I know, so many things from the past are holding us back.

Of course, experiences differ from one region to another. There are places in Canada where racism is stronger and more dangerous than others. There must also be places where cohabitation is beautiful and even strong, particularly in remote regions, isolated from the big urban centres. I'm thinking of Abitibi-Témiscamingue, in western Quebec, a region with wild, bold landscapes, violated and dishonoured

17

because it's too beautiful and too rich. Just like our daughters. Val-d'Or, but also Kitcisakik and Lac-Simon, where I've heard all kinds of frightening stories of altercations between Indigenous and non-Indigenous people. I have a feeling that the ready-made images that people have of each other have a lot to do with it. Not knowing how to say things, how to talk is what leads to a lot of conflicts. A lot of misunderstanding, a lot of silence.

I believe that on our side we have for a long time been afraid of what the dominant society has become. Seeing the power of the "White man" (which is what your people are always called in our communities), with his weapons, his diseases, his way of playing with (real) fire and destroying at an ever greater speed the whole territory that our ancestors held dear, did, of course, become very frightening. It's a little like the Windigo, the one that eats everything. But we shouldn't allow ourselves to generalize. I know that it was only a handful of people in power who built this "new" world, the world of races in a hierarchy, simply in order to have a monopoly over the resources of the territory.

Racism was born out of this relationship of domination. Man created it better to achieve his purposes. To exploit the territory and his fellow beings and have more room. To be able to take even more and impose himself. Impose his way of thinking. His way of believing in higher powers. We should remember the reason why most of the explorers came to America after its "discovery": it was for conquest. One of their tasks was to exterminate the Indigenous Peoples or to make war on them. Of course, there were exceptions, such as the French navigator and founder of Quebec City Samuel de Champlain, or the *coureurs des bois* (fur traders, literally "runners of the wood"), or all those who "converted" to Indigenous thought (whether they were of French or British origin). I believe they had understood why we were

18

so connected with the physical territory. It was to be one with nature. To taste the freedom of being in a relationship with one's environment, and not in a relationship of domination over it. To come into the world with the idea that we are only a tiny part of its giant body, which itself is a tiny part of the whole cosmos. Who are we to claim to be great? Children?

So how can we rebuild trust? Rebuild the broken, betrayed word? Sometimes everything begins with a simple thought. Which leads to another, which leads to another, and so on and so forth. We need to ask questions. At this time, I'm calling myself into question. I'm calling into question my relationship with the "White man."

I leave you with these words:
Niaut nuitsheuakan, tshima minukuamin.

Nin,
Natasha

5

Kuei, kuei, nuitsheuakan,

You're right to speak of pride. Of course, the psychology of racism is a complicated subject, perhaps as complicated as colonization itself. As you pointed out, the racist system was put in place by a handful of people in power – royalty, nobility, traders, and the church – even if we must recognize that the vast majority of Whites accepted it and participated in it. However, when we speak of racism and of colonialism, the danger is to think that Whites consist of a homogeneous group. We weren't one when colonization started, and we are not more so today; we remain diverse.

We can't forget that the majority of European colonists arrived in America in hopes of building a new life. Certain among them came to do commerce and make a profit, but many were ignorant and oppressed. We can easily imagine their fear when they arrived on this new continent where the inhabitants' culture was entirely foreign to them. Those arriving were above all concerned with survival. The desire to protect themselves and to be strong was understandable, even if the result was destructive.

However, it was thanks to Indigenous people that many of those arriving from Europe learned to survive in a challenging environment. In truth, our people were at that time closer to each other than they are today. New France's society was built not only with dialogue but also with numerous intercultural exchanges between the two peoples. The transfer of knowledge from the Indigenous people to the Whites, as well as the mixed marriages, allowed settlers to survive and establish lasting communities in the Americas. Among colonists, those from France were much closer to the Indigenous people than those from England were.

The greatest problems resulted from the individuals for whom colonialism was an expansionist project to exploit the land and people, and a means of waging war against other European powers. At that time, political and ideological conflicts divided Europe. In addition to the commercial benefits, certain White arrivals wanted to convert the planet to Christianity and impose their vision of civilization. Numerous forces converged into an extreme racism – a racism fed by ignorance, fear, and greed – and the White people in power happily made use of it to assure their domination of America.

I would like to return to the subject of pride and the fact that Whites are not a homogeneous group, even if they often believe this to be the case. It's true that pride and insecurity are linked. Based on my experiences and studies, demonstrating our power and submitting others to our will are primal urges as much in humans as in animals, and it's especially present in humans who have themselves been oppressed. Millions of Whites who wanted to survive had experienced violence and lived in insecurity. Having been abused by those in power, they in turn reproduced these abuses on those who were more vulnerable.

If those who were poorest were often (but not always) the most *overtly* racist, it's not only because of a lack of education, but also because of competition for limited resources. We see this phenomenon in many places. In the United States, for instance, impoverished Whites live in greater proximity and have more in common with African

American people of a similar economic class than they do with wealthy Whites; however, they fight between themselves for the same resources while the majority of the country's wealth accumulates in the hands of a few people – those who constitute the notorious "one percent." Here, during colonization, many impoverished French lived well alongside Indigenous people, while others saw themselves in competition with them for the control of the land and its resources.

In his book of essays, *Race Matters*, African American political activist and social critic Cornel West writes,

> *Without the presence of black people in America, European-Americans would not be "white" – they would be Irish, Italians, Poles, Welsh, and other engaged in class, ethnic, and gender struggles over resources and identity.*[3]

Here, West is speaking of the United States, but in Canada the situation was slightly more complicated, due to the historic conflict between the French and English. However, the presence of Indigenous people had a similar impact to that which he describes. The idea of being "White" allowed people to have a sense of belonging to a group on this continent, even though they were diverse in their ways of being and their ideologies. The tour de force achieved by those in power was to unite Whites by fostering a fear of the other and a desire to be "normal" – by encouraging them to play the role that the dominant culture assigned to us.

A few years ago, I read a study on "negativity" among

---

3   Cornel West, *Race Matters* (Boston: Beacon Press, 1993), 156. The words *black* and *white* are written without capitals in the original quote, contrary to our usage in this book.

humans.[4] According to it, if two people who meet for the first time speak of a third person whom they know and both like, they'll be less inclined to feel close or establish a strong bond. But if they speak of a third person whom they dislike, they'll immediately feel that they are friends. This dynamic merits consideration on the scale of collective groups: when two groups share distrust for a third group, they can easily forget their difference. In international politics, this is perhaps implied by the saying, "The enemy of my enemy is my friend." It certainly plays an important role in the perpetuation of racism, since the feeling of belonging to a group is one of the strongest human needs, deeply rooted in our biology. Rejecting an individual or a group creates a profound sense of solidarity among those who band together in opposition.

Even the conception of the relationship with nature isn't simple for Whites, since certain among us have maintained a very romantic image of Indigenous Peoples. My mother, for example, always encouraged me to understand them and to respect them, but she sometimes described them without nuance. Of course, she was herself young at that time and was speaking to a child, and today, she and many others have deepened their understanding. I mentioned this simply to emphasize that non-Indigenous people, like any other human group, are complex and have diverse cultural views.

My father, however, warned me that Indigenous people were dangerous. He told me stories about them involving violence, alcoholism, and drugs. He also told me stories of violence, alcoholism, and drugs concerning White people, without ever saying: "Whites are dangerous. Be careful!" It was as if he projected everything that he hated about

---

4   Jennifer K. Bosson et al., "Interpersonal Chemistry through Negativity: Bonding by Sharing Negative Attitudes about Others," *Personal Relationships* 13, No. 2 (June 2006), 135–150.

himself onto Indigenous people, or onto those whom he perceived as different from himself.

Ironically, my father was a criminal and a violent individual, and, during a period in my childhood, we lived in a house on a First Nations reserve in British Columbia. He dealt with Indigenous men who sold him salmon that he resold illegally on the open market. It was from them that he learned to make smoked salmon. He smoked it in old fridges that he kept in the forest, and when he sold it, he made a decent profit.

I have many memories of him having a beer with an Indigenous man. But when he was alone with me, he spoke negatively about Indigenous people, claiming that they didn't want to integrate into the "normal life" and that they were prisoners of the past. He told me similar things about people from Quebec, even though that's where he was from, and he called them "ignorant" and "backward." But when his talk concerned Indigenous people, he always added that I should be careful around them, that they weren't honest – even though he lied often, taking pains to teach me to lie. He refused to conform to many social norms and in no way lived a so-called "normal life." (It's hard to imagine a criminal preaching about honesty, is it not?) He would tell me that Indigenous people didn't like Whites. He, in any case, certainly didn't like Indigenous people.

His was a type of racism that I have heard thousands of times all over the earth, a banal and irrational racism that many humans have learned to reproduce without thinking. There was nothing exceptional about it. This is exactly what renders it so dangerous: it's a reflex that expresses itself almost without effort. Hearing it, we learn that those who are different are dangerous, and when we look at them, we perceive only what justifies this belief.

I see an ocean of complexity that could be explored in

what I have just written. I will stop here for the moment, knowing that I will need many letters to better understand these ideas. But I will continue to consider your question – "How can we rebuild trust?" – and I think that the first steps consist of deconstructing the monolithic and reductive ideas about the cultures and identities of other peoples. We're on the right path: sharing ideas and meditating on each other's words.

I look forward to reading your next letter.

Iame!
Deni

P.S. What does *tshima minukuamin* mean?

6

Kuei, kuei, nuitsheuakan,

My friend, I think that the violence that one carries inside depends not only on the experience of each person, but also on the experience of each people. Do you also believe that the history of colonization, assimilation, and genocide is now part of our DNA?

One evening, when I was sixteen years old, I came across the film *The Invisible Nation* by the Québécois singer-songwriter Richard Desjardins and filmmaker Robert Monderie.[5] I was home alone, sitting in front of the television, watching Radio-Canada, and it came on. I watched the whole thing, from beginning to end.

The film talks about Richard Desjardins's encounter with the Algonquins of Kitcisakik and Lac-Simon in Quebec's Abitibi-Témiscamingue region. A feature documentary in which Desjardins gives a voice to the residents of those two villages. In the film, they talk for the first time about their lives, the psychological, physical, and sexual violence they were subjected to in the Indian residential schools. Some of them were fifty or sixty years old when Desjardins and Monderie made the documentary. A whole lifetime keeping those secrets... A whole lifetime of being broken. Dulling

---

5   *Le peuple invisible / The Invisible Nation* (Montreal: Office national du film du Canada / National Film Board of Canada, 2001), 93 min.

the pain and the dark thoughts. The dispossession. It was being close to death that finally loosened their tongues. Those revelations were like a bombshell in the Catholic Church and in our communities. How many knew about it; how many never did?

We didn't choose to go to the residential schools. They came to get us with the Royal Canadian Mounted Police and officials from social services.

Parents were threatened with being thrown in jail or having their property confiscated if they "blocked access to education for their children." The Canadian government was pursuing a very precise goal: turn the "Indian" children into little White children. For the Canadian authorities of the time, there was no doubt that if those little Indians became Canadian citizens starting in childhood, it would only make them better adults. And above all, they wouldn't have to hear about those Indians anymore! A few years ago, the Truth and Reconciliation Commission of Canada was created in order to finally shed light on the abuses committed in those residential schools. It was given a mandate to collect as many accounts as possible from those who are now called "survivors." In total, the commissioners heard more than six thousand. (Doing a little research on the subject, a few months ago, I discovered a "Truth and Reconciliation Commission" had also been held in South Africa to heal the wounds of apartheid[6] ...)

At the very instant when, ironically, my mind was assimilating the information in the Desjardins/Monderie documentary, at that precise moment of my life, a great shift occurred in my body, in my veins, and in my head, which had a profound effect on me.

---

6   Literally "separateness" in Afrikaans. A system of institutionalized racial segregation and discrimination in South Africa between 1948 and 1991.

I understood it all. I was going through a difficult time, both personally and with my family. I couldn't understand any of it, you know. None of it. Except that from that moment on, when I became aware of the violence done to Indigenous children sent to the religious residential schools, from the 1920s to the 1990s, everything was explained. All that human misery of which I was a spectator and of which I was quietly becoming the indirect victim, since I had unconsciously inherited the wounds inflicted on my people for more than a generation.

Right away, I forgave everything. Forgave my alcoholic grandfather, my alcoholic grandmother, my difficult mother, my absent father. My teen years when I didn't understand why I had fettered myself with imaginary chains that, with time, had become unbreakable. Why so much misery, why so much pain, why so much need to shout, to cry, to get mad? The need to wound others? To wound each other?

Everything was there.

That was how I suddenly became an adult. Not necessarily in reality (I've been through so many financial and interpersonal problems over the years since) but in my mind. I was no longer a child nor a teenager. I got past my reckless attitude, even though, still today, I sometimes find that certain aspects of my personality are symptoms of old repressed wounds that I inherited when I was very young, whether or not they have healed. In fact, the city girl and the reserve girl often clash inside me.

This awakening taught me to understand and easily recognize people struggling with themselves or with their past. Or the past of their people. I came to an understanding of my own past. Since then, I fear nothing.

Recently I watched the same documentary again. Except that this time, I couldn't stand to watch it for very long. The way the narrative was constructed irritated me from the start – it seems crazy that I never saw it before! I felt it was again the cliché of the White man who lands among the natives to explain to his people who these primitives are. A way of depicting everything as a "foreign culture." Oh well. Perhaps that film was necessary at the time, to bring the subject to public attention ...

As for racism coming from the Indigenous side, it consists above all of blaming everything on the "Whites." When we talk about White people, the image that comes to mind is that of the people who came bringing us imbalance, disease, and misery, because that's the intergenerational memory that has been passed down to us, and it's the most intense. I realize – you were talking about generalization – that that image was reinforced by the residential school system. For many of our elders, the "White man" exemplifies that group of people who participated in that system of board- ing schools for children, across the country. This image is certainly very understandable, but it bothers me.

I remember a sign put up in front of a house in my native village that read: "Whites out! Liars, bastards!" I've actually heard people say that the only White people we knew on the reserve were drug dealers. People who came for the sole purpose of selling us their poison. Centuries ago, other people who came for the sole purpose of selling something led to the destruction of our territories, then our cultures, then our languages, then ... members of our communities. Today, with drugs and alcohol, we are facing another form of destruction. More internal, deeper.

This vision of the White man that I'm presenting to you, which I'm trying to summarize for you in a few words, a few phrases, is one I've shared. Of course, we absolutely must not generalize on the basis of the malicious or dis- honest actions of a few people. But sometimes, when I'm really, really angry, that vision of the other comes back to haunt me. It gnaws at my insides. Even though I always end up convincing myself that it's too easy to accuse the other, to blame the White majority, you should know that it's a daily struggle. Just like my struggle against asphalt, against materialism, against skyscrapers. And yet, it's among those elements that I see myself as a survivor, as an Innu who knows how to walk in any territory. Many of us carry what I call the "wound of colonization." Québécois have to become aware of this. Five hundred years of history is not easily forgotten. We remember. It's in our blood and in the eyes of our children. That's why we are trying to transmit light to them.

I also have to confess to you that for many years I didn't think about all that. I have just now, between two sentences, started replaying the Desjardins/Monderie film on my computer, in the background, to help me write because, sometimes, the words don't come. They need to be woken up. And now I've suddenly been shaken. Now I need to tell you that it's not my vision of the other, that I've never been racist toward those Whites I'm talking about. No. I believe that, in a way, I need to instead become reconciled with myself.

Deni, I don't know what else to tell you. What to add. You mustn't feel guilty or carry a burden that you inherited from your father. Maybe your father had Indigenous blood. Have you thought of that? And maybe that would explain the inner rage that I sense in him? That heavy, deaf rage that reminds me of something. A shadow that I perceive sometimes in our communities.

I'm not saying that your father maybe had Indigenous blood because Indigenous people have social problems. I'm simply wondering if he didn't carry in himself, in his body, all the heritage of the First Nations of the country. The wound of the physical territory.

I'm sorry, I don't mean to paint a portrait of your father. It's late, this evening, and I'm tired, carried away by my emotions.

I'll continue my reflections later, I imagine. Meanwhile, I say good night to you, Deni.

From Montreal,
Nin,
Natasha

P.S. "Tshima minukuamin" is what you say to wish someone "good night." It's not a literal translation, however. It could mean "May you sleep well," but there again ... it lacks the concept of "sleeping soundly." For me, this phrase resonates as a wish that you sleep soundly, that you will have good dreams. There.

7

Dear friend, niminu-uitsheuakan,

Thank you for sharing so much about your life. Reading your letter, I see that family is a difficult and painful subject for both of us and will require time to explore. A few years ago, I did a genetic test to learn about my ancestry and I received my results online: my genealogy was exclusively European; I had no Indigenous blood. The site (23andme.com) keeps the genetic information of thousands of people and updates it regularly based on the results of new studies, given that scientists still know relatively little about our DNA.

A few months after I received the first results, I again logged into my account to see if my genetic results had been updated. I saw that there were more traits listed (for example, my potential for hereditary diseases and my type of ear wax), and then I clicked on the section for my ancestry: the places of origin for my ancestors had become more precise, and I now was listed as having 0.5% Indigenous DNA. A year later, that amount had increased, and today it is 1.9%. I'll be curious to see if that changes in five years! But all this is to say that, yes, my father had Indigenous roots.

I recall once asking my grandmother in Quebec if we had "Indian blood." She replied that, no, we didn't have any. But then, after a moment of reflection, she added that my grandfather had cousins in New Brunswick who "walked like Indians." I suspect that this meant that they didn't walk heavily, on the heel, like those accustomed to wearing boots, but on the front of the foot, having learned to walk silently and without a thick sole. Later, my grandmother told me that my grandfather had almost no hair on his torso. She always found this to be strange and wondered if it resulted from an Indigenous inheritance. My grandfather was dark, with brown skin, and his hair was black, like that of many Québécois.

Of course, many Québécois have Indigenous blood. Thousands of European men arrived in the Saint Lawrence Valley and had children with Indigenous women. But once a society perceived as Catholic and European established itself in America, its institutions pushed colonists to identify as White and deny their Indigenous roots.

A few years ago, I read that there were numerous conflicts in Manitoba between Indigenous and non-Indigenous communities, and a great deal of racism against Indigenous people. But when the province changed its laws to allow those who had a certain percentage of Indigenous blood to hunt out of season, thousands of non-Indigenous people suddenly showed proof of sufficient Indigenous heritage to claim this status, even those who were racist toward Indigenous people.

I would like to return to the subject of my father. He had a powerful desire to belong to the dominant group, and very clearly wanted to be rich and anglophone. He was proud and had renounced his Québécois roots to live in English Canada. He hated the Catholic Church and told me about the cruelty of its priests. He would describe how few opportunities he'd had as a child, how closed the horizon had seemed. His pride was immense and his insecurity as well. I suspect that he'd felt so powerless, so trapped by poverty when he was young that he'd gone on to try to dominate everyone he met. It's conceivable that he was incapable of feeling sympathy for Indigenous people because their way of living in many ways resembled his own. Or maybe, like many people who've experienced oppression, he preferred to blame the oppressed and identify with those in power. It may even have been the case that he saw the oppression the Québécois had experienced at the hands of anglophones as similar, in certain ways, to that which Indigenous people had suffered, and he wanted to dissociate himself entirely from those who had been dominated.

Many people adopt such psychological strategies when there's a great deal of suffering in their pasts. Like many Québécois, my family hates talking about the hardships they've experienced. Mentioning certain struggles is nearly taboo. I think that Québécois have more in common with Indigenous people than they realize, but that their suffering recalls their own pasts. Maybe, one day, these similarities will serve as a foundation for compassion and mutual comprehension.

Tshima minukuamin,
Deni

P.S. And *nin*? What does it mean?

8

Kuei Deni,

Nin means "me." *Nin tshia*, "I am." I am and I speak. I write
to you. Me, Natasha.
"They walked like Indians."
I love that image. This phrase, this designation recalls
the stories and legends that inhabit the imaginary and
cultural territory of Quebec like something distant and
otherworldly.
"They walked like Indians."
How great is that? An image of people walking, who
know how to walk, that time when people knew how to
respect the earth, the territories of America, who dreamed
of it the way they would dream of the women of their lives
that they had not yet met. For some of those *coureurs des
bois* I am referring to, the lands were those women in their
lives for whom they had been waiting for a long time.
You know, not so long in the past, but far enough still
(maybe it goes back to the grandparents of my grandparents), at the time when spirituality was an integral part of
daily life, among the Innuat (plural of *Innu*), couples had a
precise form. In the traditional couple, there was the hunter
man and the clan woman. The clan was matrilineal. Our
spirituality was animist. Joséphine Bacon, a marvellous poet
you've certainly heard of, Innu from Pessamit like me, often
tells her audience that in those days, the woman prepared

her husband's ceremonial clothes when he left to go hunting. The belief was that a Woman of Space lived in the hunting territories, the Nutshimit. She was the Spirit of the territory. She was in direct contact with the master spirits of the animals, herds, and flocks of birds. So the women dressed their men in their finest to meet the Woman of Space. The innushkueuat (Innu women) dreamed of those clothes at night and, in the daytime, they made the fabrics. If they dreamed of patterns, they drew them on the coats the next day. Their men had to be good-looking and please the Woman of Space to ensure a good hunt for the whole community. If the women were successful, the men came back with lots of game. And everyone celebrated, they did the "makushan," to give thanks to each spirit that had accompanied the hunters and watched over the clan too. Each generation learned to be grateful for what it obtained to ensure that their good fortune would continue.

Personally I believe that a lot of Québécois have no idea of their ancient heritage. I don't mean Indigenous heritage. Well, maybe yes, in the sense of the French word *autochtone*, which means "sprung from the land itself." I want to mainly talk about the heritage of the territory itself. Memory, the transmission of the environment to human beings. Oddly, I discovered, by searching on the Internet for the definition of *autochtone*, that, in Greek mythology, *autokhthōn* meant a child born spontaneously out of the earth, without parents. If the Indigenous people of the Americas are children born spontaneously from the earth, without parents, that means they need to be tamed, adopted. It's not for nothing, I imagine, that the "Indians" of the time were called "the children" of the Queen of England. Spelled out in black and white.

A heritage is a door to freedom. I'm not sure that the Indigenous heritage that is talked about so much in the media, social networks, and the films that are currently being made about Quebec identity absolutely has to be connected to furs, snowshoes, glass beads, and *ceintures fléchées*[7] ... If war broke out tomorrow, if the country was levelled by forest fires, if the cities were destroyed, what would remain of that identity? What would happen to that heritage?

I also believe that heritage resides in the perceptions and concepts of the universe that the earlier generations have transmitted to us. Isn't the idea of knowledge indissociable from that of transmission? But coming to terms with one's individual heritage and assuming one's collective heritage are two different things we could reflect on together. Like the Métis, who, at the time, realized that a lot of them had a father of European origin and an Indigenous mother, and so they decided to come together to proclaim themselves a "people." They were conscious of the cultural wealth that their double origin enabled them to bring together, to share. So the question arises: if the Québécois realize they have an Indigenous heritage, a heritage from the earth, more significant than what they thought, what can we do with that heritage? Which artefacts, which ways of thinking could we bring together to better unite us and complete us?

In your last letter, you told me about your grandmother's comment about your grandfather regarding the colour of his skin and his hair. My reaction was to find that as normal as could be! We, among the Innuat, see it in the eyes of many Québécois. We immediately recognize eyes that are familiar to us. We look alike. Last April, when I was at a writing residency in Chicoutimi, in Quebec's Saguenay–Lac-Saint-Jean region, I went to cafés to work. It was the first time that I had spent so much time in the region. I'd never noticed how much Québécois had Indigenous

---

7   Ceintures fléchées, also called arrow sashes, Assomption sashes, or voyageur sashes, are colourful, long woven sashes that are traditionally worn by the French Canadians and the Métis since the late 1700s.

features as obvious as black hair, thick eyebrows, almond-shaped eyes, high cheekbones. Of course, not everyone matched that description, but the majority of the people I encountered possessed those "marks of time." There was so much mixing in Saguenay–Lac-Saint-Jean. The Innuat themselves have the blood of French Canadians, Scots, the Irish, the Abenaki, the Maliseet. And yet, even though each of us carries the blood of the other, there is still a lot of racism between Indigenous and non-Indigenous people in remote regions.

You wrote that "Maybe, one day, these similarities will serve as a foundation for compassion and mutual comprehension." I firmly believe that. I believe that from this point forward, becoming aware of the history of our relationships and raising questions about their current state, about the circumstances that led to this state of affairs, will be the first foundations of what we can set in motion in the public space, through social networks, the media, schools, etc.

One day, perhaps, Québécois will remember or understand what it means really means to "walk like an Indian." Walk in their shoes. I believe that the day will come soon when the "Indians" invite the "Whites" to make a journey with them. And the latter will perhaps notice that it is comfortable to walk in shoes that don't imprison the feet. Shoes that are adapted to the territory, shaped by it. And that brings them freedom.

> *They walked like Indians*
> *on the path of reparation*
> *time will tell us*
> *time will tell us*
> *if they follow the right path.*

... if we find the right path together with those letters, my friend.

See you soon.
Tshima minukuamin kie tshin,
Natasha

P.S. Okay, I'm going to add an answer: *kie tshin* means "you too." I had said to you *nin* for "me"; *tshin* is "you" and *tshinanu* "we together."

9

Dear Natasha,

You are right. The Québécois are far from being French and their identity is intimately linked with those of Indigenous people. It's perhaps time to celebrate our mixing and to build new ways of seeing ourselves and our pasts so as to better integrate our Indigenous heritage.

Since my grandmother spoke to me about the family cousins who "walked like Indians," I have spent a good deal of time watching how people walk in many countries. I went so far as to do some research on the subject – more precisely on our way of running – and I learned that running played an important role in the evolution of humans. According to a scientific theory, humans evolved as they are today (with long legs and very little body hair) so that they can hunt while running, since very few species have the endurance to run as we do. Studies have shown that humans never ran on their heels before the invention of the thick sole used in running shoes over the last half-century. We ran on the ball of the foot so that we wouldn't injure ourselves, but also so that we'd be more agile. If we try to walk in the forest without the protection of thick soles, we are all obliged to "walk like Indians." If not, we make too much noise and hurt ourselves. In countries around the world, I've seen people who walk and run "like Indians." The only ones who don't do this are those who wear soles sufficiently thick to insulate themselves from the earth. Studies also show that the thicker the sole is, the more the many small muscles in our feet atrophy and the more likely we are to injure ourselves.[8]

Since my last letter, I have continued thinking about the question of similarities between our cultures and I have realized that, in order to understand each other, we have to explore the differences that exist between our backgrounds. I wrote that the Québécois have more in common with Indigenous people than they realize and that their suffering reminds them of their own past. Both groups struggled against the British Empire to preserve their identity; both experienced hardship and poverty, even if the Québécois progressively affirmed themselves as a distinct people and have taken positions of power that have, in turn, placed them in the position of colonizers in relationship to Indigenous people. The Québécois colonialism that exists today has increasingly less of a strong political bent, taking place primarily by economic means and the imposition of culture and social values.

Despite the similarities we've discussed, it's extremely important to highlight that the traumas experienced by both groups are not of the same nature and intensity. We often speak of changes that we would like to see, but we have yet to learn to speak intelligently about past traumas. When you

---

8   Examples of such studies include: Hannah M. Rice, Steve T. Jamison, and Irene S. Davis, "Footwear Matters: Influence of Footwear and Foot Strike on Load Rates During Running," *Medicine and Science in Sports and Exercise* 48, No. 12 (2016), 2462–68, https://doi.org/10.1249/MSS.0000000000001030; Richard Withnall, Joanne Eastaugh, and Nick Freemantle, "Do shock absorbing insoles in recruits undertaking high levels of physical activity reduce lower limb injury? A randomized controlled trial," *Journal of the Royal Society of Medicine* 99, No. 1 (January 2006), 32–37, https://insights.ovid.com /crossref?an=00005305-200601000-00012. Additional information can be found in online articles published in recent years by *The Guardian*, *Runner's World*, and *The Atlantic*.

described your family, I had a clearer sense of the impact of trauma across generations. In the United States, I have often heard Whites say that their families worked hard for self-betterment, and I have heard them ask why African American people haven't achieved as much. I have heard Québécois speak in the same way of Indigenous people.

But this is obviously too simplistic. Whites have to recognize the degree to which our society actively destroyed Indigenous families. Recently, I was reading a book by Bev Sellars, the Chief of the Xatśūll First Nation, in British Columbia. Its title is *They Called Me Number One*, since, when she lived in a residential school, this was the number she received and had to use as her name all through her childhood.[9] Her teachers didn't use her real name, only the number. She explains that all of her family members, including her grandparents, remembered their numbers from the residential schools, even decades later. She describes the violence there, and explains that she was at school with several of her brothers and sisters, but since they weren't the same age, they were assigned to different groups and almost never saw each other. In the dorms, they didn't have permission to seek comfort from each other, and they saw their parents only during the summer and the Christmas break. They nearly became strangers.

The importance of family for social stability is immense. White people who don't have stable families can at least feel a certain belonging to the larger society and a sense of acceptance. Inversely, many minorities have interiorized the knowledge that, even if they make an effort, they won't be accepted, or rather that they must make significantly more effort than White people to obtain a fraction of the

---

9   Bev Sellars, *They Called Me Number One: Secrets and Survival at an Indian Residential School* (Vancouver: Talonbooks, 2012).

respect that White people automatically receive. A number of studies have shown the effect of discouragement on individuals – how much this feeling can undermine a person's ambitions.[10]

As you said, trauma leaves a cellular memory. It leaves its traces in our genes, and it lives in our bodies. Healing from a broken family – I can attest to this myself – takes time. But healing from generations of destroyed families, generations of fathers and mothers who saw their children stolen by the government, who felt that they weren't respected by society, who were raped and systematically abused because their origins weren't European: how is it possible? It's difficult for me to imagine the challenges people must overcome before they can begin to rebuild.

In terms of what White people can do – we can stop blaming victims for the pain they experience. I have too often heard White people say that Indigenous people or African American people should leave their suffering in the past and change their lives, as if this was a simple decision. That understanding of the situation is cerebral and fails to recognize that trauma is experienced viscerally. We can want to forget a trauma, and we might even succeed in doing so, but it remains in us, as part of us. Even if Indigenous people were to try forgetting, White society would remind them.

Those who offer easy solutions and repeat reductive statements about race fail to recognize that our wounds can paralyze us. I value the power of the imagination, and believe that we must take the time to learn about and imagine the lives of others. Without doing so, we will

---

10   See, for example: Robin Nicole Johnson-Ahorlu, "The Academic Opportunity Gap: How Racism and Stereotypes Disrupt the Education of African American Undergraduates," *Race, Ethnicity and Education* 15, No. 5 (2012), 633–52, https://doi.org/10.1080/13613324.2011.645566.

speak of them without recognizing the brutal impact that our words can have on them.

Natasha, in an earlier letter, we spoke of silence, but you aren't silent. Your wounds haven't left you without words. You are an artist in many domains – a writer, a poet, an actor, and also an activist. How did you find the strength to speak and to share your experiences?

And in your last letter, you wrote that my father's rage reminded you of something – a shadow that you sometimes perceive in your community. What is your experience and understanding of that shadow?

I have so many questions. I suppose this is the reason for our epistolary exchange.

Iame uenapissish,
Deni

10

Kuei, Deni,

I was very silent for many years. I didn't laugh very often, and when I did I would laugh loudly. I cried a lot when I was a teenager. You might say that's not so unusual, that everybody whines at that age. I don't believe it. Deni, I cried a lot. I didn't know what was hidden deep down inside me, except that it was an invisible weight and, in my moments of distress, fatigue, and anxiety, it made me sob through the nights as a young girl. When I run into other young people from the reserve with those dark circles under their eyes, I remember the darkness I knew before I started to look for the light.

In those times of silent weeping, I dreamed a lot about my future life. I wanted to become a singer. I already saw myself, heard myself singing. I already saw the stages, the audiences. I also told myself that one day, maybe I would write, but later, when I was over thirty. Maybe. Then one day, I decided I wanted to paint. So I painted, I saw myself becoming a world-famous painter. That dream has remained deeply rooted inside me. I had made the decision to follow that dream. I longed to improve myself. Deep inside me, I felt that I had the power to achieve this.

The power of dreams is undeniable. I can tell you something about it. If I hadn't had such great expectations of the future, such crazy hopes, I don't know what would have become of me. I don't even know if I would still be alive! Because there are still times when I feel profoundly discontent with my life, for no apparent reason. Each time, I tell myself that I've been lucky to have discovered ways of expressing myself that have permitted me to exorcize my demons, those of my parents and my grandparents, as well as those inherited from colonization. Today, I'm very conscious of those wounds and, even though I don't know those of my forebears, I'm aware that I carry them inside me. I'm already beginning to reflect on them in order to tame them and, with time, I hope to be able to live with them from day to day. To be able one day to figure it all out, too. As for dreams, we have to spread the idea that they're possible, that they simply require a lot of courage and that, when we search for ourselves, life does the rest. Just as soon as, to get through it, we shake it up a little. To get out of the darkness.

I can't explain why I talk so much, why I express myself so much. Except, perhaps, precisely when I take history into account. The history of the First Nations. Not only the history that we lament – colonization, genocide, residential schools – but also the history of resistance. The story of standing up for ourselves. The insurrections. The roadblocks. It flows in my veins just as much. I believe that my name is resilience.

I believe I have finally found that resilience that seems to be transmitted in the blood through my inner distress. I finally did theatre, because it was also one of my great desires. At the time, I was very introverted and I told myself that the dramatic arts might be good for me. When I was in high school, at a certain moment I started refusing to do any oral presentations in class!

I can't explain either how I never fell into using hard drugs. I easily could have. I wasn't very far from it. I was never tempted by them, and what frightened me were the effects they could have on my body.

I believe that, in life, you have to set yourself certain times to face your demons. The shadow I'm talking to you about is that intention that was at the origin of the creation of reserves. A vile, genocidal, alienating intention. It is often said that it's the intention that counts. And the intention remains, whatever the actions that have been taken subsequently. After, a collective amnesia was fabricated among the Québécois, erasing the Indigenous presence from the history of the country. An amnesia planned by the governments. And we live with that idea: of being erased, forgotten, incarcerated … Some have even come to believe, without anyone asking them to, that they should erase themselves. What a strange idea! Why renounce existence? How could that intention of "killing the Indian in the child" have become so instilled in the minds of a people? We're carrying so much historical baggage in our genes! How can you forget your own blood? Your own memory! We carry on our skin the scars of the bullets received by our ancestors. We carry the memory of those disputes.

During the Oka Crisis, in the summer of 1990, people tried to discredit the Indigenous activists and not the Canadian military, while we were all going the wrong way on the road of the Mohawk cemetery. The wrong way, except maybe for the fact of standing up for ourselves, in the famous pines, between the birch and the tamarack, haunted by the memory of a bullet that strayed into the body of a single White man. But they never talk about that Mohawk elder, Joe Armstrong, who died of heart failure after being stoned by a mob of Québécois! They only talk about that corporal and those who are now supposed to be treated like wild dogs with no rights. A few have, in fact, remained very radical, perched in the tree of their anger, of their dishonour. If they sometimes speak loudly and strongly it's because they have not been listened to – although that they've also sometimes been rebuffed by their brothers and sisters.

We're afraid. We're all afraid. So we keep our mouths shut. We keep quiet.

Because, sometimes, there's nothing more to say, nothing more to do. Sometimes, it's because we know that the best is yet to come.

Hugs,
Natasha

P.S. I really get fired up when I'm writing to you! I have to remind myself that all these things light a fire inside me and it requires a lot of oxygen! History needs to be rewritten and I hope we'll know how to write it, my friend. I hope that these pages will burn away our wounds so they can heal better. I believe the work has begun.

11

Dear Maikaniss,

Tell me about this name. On Facebook, I see that you also call yourself Maikaniss. Where did you receive this name? What does it mean to you?

Since reading your letter, I've thought a great deal about Joe Armstrong, the Mohawk elder who was injured by the stoning and who died. I recall having seen the attack on television when I was fifteen: the rocks shattered the windows of the cars driven by the Indigenous people who were simply trying to leave the reserve and the police stopped their cars and did nothing to protect the women, children, and elderly in them. All this because the town of Oka wanted to enlarge a golf course and build condos on the lands of the Mohawk people – the Kanien'kehá:ka people, to use the name Mohawks choose for themselves – who'd already lost so much. All this for money and profit.

I've also thought a great deal about empathy, about the imagination and the written word – and their power to help build connections between people. I ask myself often what we can do to expand our empathy, to feel the pain of the other and act for the collective good. Maybe those questions are too idealistic, but the lack of empathy for others is flagrant.

I remember the American invasion of Iraq in 2003, and the televised spectacle of the bombs falling on buildings in Baghdad. Some Americans I knew were awed, as if they were watching a Hollywood blockbuster. They laughed as they said that they'd never seen anything like it. They didn't appear aware that they were the audience for the destruction of homes and workplaces – spaces cherished by humans like themselves. They seemed to lack the awareness that the people of Iraq love their homes, their cities, and their country just as we love our own. At that moment, the reaction of Americans showed me that – perhaps unconsciously – they didn't consider the Iraqi people as humans. In the words of the British writer George Orwell, author of *Nineteen Eighty-Four* and *Animal Farm*, they saw them as "unpeople." Today, in the news headlines, when we speak of people who are killed on earth, we exclude the vast majority of those who aren't White. The suffering of these non-people is of least importance to us. It constitutes a menace to the social order that we've established. If we begin to ask questions about their suffering, we would be obliged to question the foundations of our societies, and few White Westerners are prepared to do that.

Is this not the same process that was at work in the case of Joe Armstrong and the families who wanted to leave the reserve during the Oka Crisis? Many Québécois have said to me: "But the Mohawks closed the highway!" As if the frustration that resulted from that justified violence. Or they have told me about the death of one of the police officers in the standoff, as if the death of one justified the death of another. If an angry Indigenous person had broken the windows of a White family – even for revenge – and a White person died, the assailant would still be in prison. There is good evidence for me to believe this. In Canada, more than a quarter of the people in federal prisons are

Indigenous, even though they constitute less than 5% of the country's population.[11]

The Oka Crisis was a story of rage. Few Québécois understood and respected the anger behind the actions of the Indigenous people involved there. They thought only of their own short-term desires (the opening of the highway) even though they should have considered the origins of the problem and looked for a lasting solution. What would have been the result of that crisis if the Québécois had turned their frustration against the government to demand a true change in attitudes toward Indigenous people? Instead, they attacked those who were most vulnerable.

It's in this way that those who hold the power retain their influence. They divide those who are least wealthy and who are most vulnerable in society with the result that they must struggle among themselves for resources. This social dynamic has played a significant role in the history of conflicts between impoverished Whites and African Americans in the United States. Poor Whites identify with rich Whites who control the country, without realizing that the latter don't act in their favour.

Thousands of books have shed light on this social dynamic without our society having made the necessary changes. The English essayist Sydney Smith is quoted as having said: "Never try to reason the prejudice out of a man. It was not reasoned into him, and cannot be reasoned out." In other words, we are emotional creatures, and our beliefs – as well as our prejudices – often arise from our emotional responses. We first have the emotional responses

---

11   Raphaël Bouvier-Auclair, "Présence record d'Autochtones dans les pénitenciers canadiens [Record presence of Indigenous people in Canadian penitentiaries]," Radio-Canada, January 14, 2016, http://ici.radio-canada.ca /nouvelle/759568/autochtone-prison-peine-minimale-penitencier-canada-prison.

and then try to rationalize them so that we can believe they are right. To better understand the experiences of Indigenous people, White people should read and listen to their stories.

In your last letter, you wrote:

> *Some have even come to believe, without anyone asking them to, that they should erase themselves. What a strange idea! Why renounce existence? How could that intention of "killing the Indian in the child" have become so instilled in the minds of a people?*

The last sentence refers to the residential schools, and, in the forward to Bev Sellars's book, Chief Bill Wilson references the character observed in many Indigenous people of his generation – "shyness, nervousness, and a subservient attitude." He explains that only in learning about the residential schools did he understand the origins of this temperament. The Whites in power succeeded at inculcating in their Indigenous students the idea that they should erase themselves. Perhaps the students who succeeded in doing so experienced less sexual abuse and violence than the others. Perhaps the traumas they experienced discouraged and demoralized them. In listening to your stories and those of other Indigenous people, I feel the weight of colonial history. The experiences and suffering of all those individuals are less and less abstract: I begin to feel them in the way that we feel all stories and history to which we open ourselves.

It's for this reason that analyzing a situation isn't enough; we have to humanize it. We have to invite others to understand our lives and our ways of experiencing the world, just as the writer invites the reader to enter into their universe,

with their vision of existence and all their images, memories, fears, and hopes.

I will hold on to this idea for my next letter, as I await
yours. I already feel that the histories and experiences that
you have told me are inhabiting me more and more.

Iame, nuitsheuakan!
Deni

12

Dear Deni,

I'm going to have to find a name in Innu that suits you. Except I'm going to wait until I get to know you a little better. Your Innu name will come on its own. If not in this book, it will happen later.

Maikaniss means "young wolf." I wasn't given that name. I remember that when I created my Facebook account, I was looking for something other than my given name, Natasha, to maintain some degree of privacy, although most people give their real name. I also remember that during that period, I was becoming aware of my roots and I very much regretted never having received a first name in my mother tongue. And since I've dreamed of that animal since I was very little, I wanted to give my soul a name that suggested all its characteristics. It may sound funny to you, but it's true! No kidding.

Maikan is the Innu word for "wolf." We have a certain fascination for wolves. Our relationships with the animals have always been very strong. At one time, the animals spoke to us and taught us principles about human beings, as well as deep knowledge about the environment and the universe.

Deni! You were fifteen years old in 1990! And I hadn't even been born. When you write about the Oka Crisis, I can see very clearly in my head the sadly powerful images that you're referring to, because I consulted archives several times during the last three years. Oddly, when I talk about it, when I tell myself for the thousandth time that story in my head, I again feel the shocks, as if I had experienced the events. I know by heart the date when the shooting started in the pines of Oka. It was July 11, 1990. Those are also the most famous images of the crisis. I was born on March 14, 1991. Eight months later, by C-section. I don't know why I'm telling you that. The way I came into the world might explain all this burning sensation that I feel, my way of being in this world.

The Oka Crisis, the Oka Crisis, the Oka Crisis ... It has been an obsession of mine since I first heard about it. I feel it under my skin. It represents so many things to me. So much evidence of ignorance and the resulting misunderstandings. We have a long way to go. Because, since then, we have all regressed so much. At the same time, it also embodies the mentalities of the period. I wasn't even born when it took place and it's part of me. I was born with it.

The Crisis began when the Kanien'kehá:ka (Mohawk) of Kanehsatà:ke (Kanesatake) wanted to stop a development project on their ancestral territory – of which the reserve represents only one fifth – according to what the Crown "bequeathed" to them in the Royal Proclamation of 1763. That's what's happened with all the ancestral territories of our peoples in North America. It was, they said, to better organize relationships with the Amerindians.

They never tell the history of the resistance by the Indigenous Peoples since the beginning of colonization in the Americas. Because they don't know that history. However, it should be recorded in the collective memory. Many rebellions took place in the course of our history. They have marked our imaginary and are today the source of our pride in our identity. Government agents have often infiltrated Indigenous resistance groups to discredit them, both with the general population and with politicians. There are reasons why certain preconceived ideas about Indigenous resistance are still expressed in public!

I'm not saying that we're proud of the violence we have used until now in certain situations that are called "crises." Violence is never a solution, but I believe that it has since the beginning marked the relationships that the conquerors wanted to establish with us. After, it became a protective reflex. We were dispossessed and so often, we were deceived, betrayed, insulted; all these gestures sometimes cause a build-up of a kind of violence, a rage that can become enormous … But those events today feed the courage that we lacked in the past to impose our limitations in our relationships with non-Indigenous people.

There was a first attempt by the Taíno people, in Haiti and the Dominican Republic, to eliminate the first settlers; all those Christopher Columbuses, Gonzalo Guerreros, Gil Gonzálezes, and Nicolás de Ovandos. The Europeans massacred the Taíno. The Haitians tell the fascinating story of Queen Anacaona, the "Golden Flower," their demigoddess, a *cacique* (chief) who had a large army under her command. She was a poet and a prophet. The conquistadores accused her of scheming to exterminate them and she was hanged. Then they put the whole of Fort La Navidad to fire and sword, before Columbus came back from his first return journey to Europe.

There was resistance by the Maya, who tried to repel the Spanish who had come with González. The Europeans had firearms.

There was the Zapatista uprising in Chiapas, Mexico.

There were rebellions by Pontiac, the Haida on the West Coast, the American Indian Movement.

That last movement, born in the early 1970s, led to the imprisonment of the legendary Leonard Peltier. He'd been

56

charged with the death of two FBI agents. And, well, that story is more than forty years old and Peltier is still in prison. No proof of his guilt was ever provided.

The Oka Crisis.

How many blockades and barricades on the roads, on the railways; how many occupations, such as the occupation of Alcatraz Island in the late 1960s, and the Lakota standoff at Wounded Knee, South Dakota, in the early 1970s? There have been so many instances of resistance that it's impossible to list them all. Territorial claims by the Algonquins in Quebec's La Vérendrye Park. The blockade by the Innuat of Route 138 on the North Shore in 2012. That last one, taking place in my native region, made me fully aware of the territory and the environmental health that we are losing every day, millimetre by millimetre. Those territories and that environment are the foundation of our identity. This is what was passed down to us over the generations by our ancestors, the conviction that the territory forges our languages, our cultures, our spiritualities. My poetry, my being, my song. My life. My cry. I embrace the earth because it is my body, just as I embrace my body when I feel threatened by any kind of danger.

I'm telling you just part of everything I know! And still, it's only a tiny part of what I should know. I'm telling it to you because these are things that affect me. They affect me because they're powerful. They symbolize our resilience. They symbolize the fact that we're ready to die to preserve what we have left of what we have known. What remains of what we are.

I'm not telling you about the past because we're nostalgic. It's just that we still have vivid memories of it. It's a great wound that can't be silenced, that won't leave us in peace. Otherwise you never would have heard about us. We remember because we've transmitted the memory among ourselves. Or if we forget it for a time, the memory always comes back by itself. This is something I know about. We remember that we were worthy. That we had societies. There was a balance in our societies that had been built up over years and generations, based on respect of the self and the other, on individual freedom. I'm not saying those societies were perfect, I'm simply explaining to you on what basis they were founded.

When I was a child, I was not taught the defining elements of my culture. No one transmitted to me what we were before the priests arrived to preach the good news to us – the bad news being that Hell exists. That's what they believed! But they convinced us of it too. And, in the end, they were right. Hell came with firearms and bulldozers. Hell came with the natural resources extraction companies. With the residential schools. Hell came, but it didn't swallow us completely. We're still here. We're still alive. We survived. And if we were swept into Hell, well, we got out not as the living dead, but very much as the living alive. More alive than ever.

You know, rebellions, revolts, the shouts rising at the precise instant when the survival instinct resurfaces. Just before dying, the breathing speeds up, brings us back to life. When I realized that I was no longer speaking my mother tongue, that I knew nothing of the people of my village, I understood that I had to find redemption. And it's that instinct that brought me to poetry. To you. To this book.

So why build golf courses in cemeteries that are cherished as the resting places of our ancestors? Can you tell me that?

I hope I can find peace.

I hope my ancestors can find peace.

Hugs.
Until our next letter,
Natasha

13

Kuei, nuitsheuakan,

I like the story behind your Facebook name. In many countries that have experienced colonization, people have again started using their traditional names. In the Congo, for example, almost everyone has two names: one in French and one in Lingala, Swahili, or the language of their region – and there are many! When I learned the name of my friends in Lingala, I was immediately reminded of their history. A name holds so much resonance. Recently, I added my mother's name to my own. One day, I realized that my name represented only half of my heritage. Even though my mother had raised me and encouraged me to be a writer (a career that my father opposed), her name was nowhere on my books or articles, or in my life. She'd always kept her maiden name, Ellis, and I recently took it as my middle name to honour her: Deni Ellis Béchard. We are all hybrids in one way or another, but we generally follow society's norms without giving them much thought. Most people use their father's surname and identify with one or another "racial group" even if our origins and cultures are diverse. We rarely acknowledge that we could live differently – that we could, for instance, change how we define our collective identity in order to open it to more people. But to do that, we would have to include the points of view of those who have been marginalized. We would have to respect their vision of the world, regardless of how much it differs from our own.

Since reading your last letter, I have been asking myself why, even today, it is so difficult for White people to give full consideration to Indigenous ways of seeing the world. I sense that this is a question we will continue to explore. Last night, I was thinking about what we have already written, trying to imagine solutions for the lack of comprehension and respect that separate people. I can imagine that there are as many solutions as our creativity would allow. The first step would be to publicly express a genuine desire to work together and to resolve problems. But we are afraid. Perhaps we fear losing our position of power. We are intent on protecting what we have and don't want to risk losing our comfort. We protect what we value and we fail to empathize with those whom we perceive as a threat to our way of life, or to our conception of history.

We will need many letters to discuss solutions, but empathy is an important subject. We must first ask what limits our empathy. Biologically, empathy allows humans to function better in groups. If we can identify with each other's emotions, we are more likely to act for the welfare of the group. But when, psychologically, we exclude people from our group, we feel little empathy for them. And according to certain studies, the more wealth people have, the less they feel compassion.[12] This is perhaps because rich people are more isolated (we live in a society in which people who have more resources can more easily isolate themselves) or perhaps because we have less need for empathy when we have power. In our evolution, we aren't far from great apes, and, even among the latter, those who are weaker

---

12   Daisy Grewal, "How Wealth Reduces Compassion," *Scientific American*, April 10, 2012, https://www.scientificamerican.com/article/how-wealth-reduces -compassion/.

must work the hardest to belong to conform to the group for the sake of protection.

It's important to point out, however, that empathy isn't a magical solution to our problems, even though it is often spoken of in that way. Rather, it must be cultivated in the same way that our other faculties require development. It cannot replace laws that protect people, or rational discussions on how to guarantee human rights for everyone.

In the beginning of this letter, I mentioned imagination and the written word. The cognitive psychologist Steven Pinker, in his book *The Better Angels of Our Nature*, which examines the decrease of violence relative to the percentage of the population over time,[13] proposes that literature, among many other factors, may have played a role in the decline of human aggression. Literature gives us access to the interior lives of others and allows us to perceive different ways of seeing the world. If we had known the story of the Mohawk elder, Joe Armstrong – all that he'd hoped and dreamed, all that he'd suffered and lost – if we had experienced this through the intimacy of words, how could we have failed to feel empathy and compassion?

If young White Québécois and Mohawks began to write to each other and exchange perspectives, would we succeed in creating a unified society in which Whites would see Mohawks as valued members, in which they wouldn't reduce them to stereotypes each time one of them made a mistake, and in which our hopes for a successful society would include their happiness and fulfillment? Would Indigenous people realize that there are thousands of Whites who want them to be happy and who hope to understand their lives?

During the recent years of recession and economic

---

13   Steven Pinker, *The Better Angels of Our Nature: Why Violence Has Declined* (New York: Viking Books, 2011).

austerity, people have worked hard to survive and have had less time for reading and intellectual reflection. And yet we must persist in creating dialogue and not intensifying the isolation. Reading is a way of listening. While reading your words, I recognize myself. How many people have had dreams similar to yours? Thousands, if not billions. The differences between us are small and yet rich. If we listen to each other, we will inevitably live more fully in this world. And if we ignore each other, we will be diminished.

Reading, listening, and even feeling empathy for others doesn't demand that we always agree. We can want the best for someone without sharing their point of view. But it's essential to recognize that their point of view exists and that they cherish it and have reasons for doing so.

It is difficult to feel respect for others when they do not respect our way of seeing life. When we disagree, we tend to refuse to listen, and, at that moment, all solutions become impossible. In truth, we fail to recognize how radical an experiment it would be to listen without judging and to respect points of view that are foreign to us.

Perhaps what I am saying seems simple or even simplistic. I see this. But few people succeed in doing what I describe. We speak in each other's place. We explain how Indigenous people think without knowing anything about them. We give priority to our values and our interests without even realizing that we are doing so.

One solution is that you continue telling your story. How do you say, "I look forward to reading more of your words"?

Iame uenapissish,
Deni

14

Kuei, nuitsheuakan,

I don't know if the verb *to read* exists in the Innu language. I'll research that.

Certain words and phrases that describe actions that we weren't familiar with, such as to read a book, are borrowed directly from French. Plus there are interpretations. But when I think about the verb *to read*, nothing in Innu-aimun (the Innu language's name in Innu) comes to mind for me. Everything depends on the context: read a book, read signs, read codes, read the stars (even then, it would instead be "to consult the stars"). You also have to know if the subject is animate or inanimate (alive or not alive). We usually create words according to the images they generate, or the actions they are used to describe, or the emotional impact they have on people. There are so many nuances – essential nuances – that I'm going to have to do research.

In recent years, I've had the same questions about my first family name, Kanapé, as you had about your mother's name. In my official documents, my name is written "Canapé." However, as I was making a gradual return to my native village, I realized that some of my distant relatives wrote their names with a *K*. And without an acute accent on the *e*. One day, someone explained to me that the name came from the Innu-aimun word *Kanapeusht*, which means "the brave one." I was told that my maternal great-grandfather Georges was the first one to receive that name. "Kanapeusht Shaush," as one would actually say in Innu. The brave Georges. It was only when the missionaries began to register the Innuat in the community schools – or simply in the band list or the government Indian Register – that we had to have a name on paper. The authorities finally francized our name, which became "Canapé." However, elsewhere on the Lower North Shore, you find surnames and first names such as Kanapeo, Mestenapeo, Kanapeush. Hearing "Kanapé" also reminds me of my maternal grandfather, André, who was an "*homme de bois*," a "man of the woods," as the Québécois say. A hunter, a solitary man, a wild bear. He had his camp, not very far from the village, in the forest, between Route 138 and the Saint Lawrence River. My happy memories of childhood are connected to that little camp, that little house built by hand by "Nimushum." *Nimushum* is the word for "my grandfather."

So I decided to write "Kanapé" with a *K* as a pen name. In order to preserve that memory in a way, but in particular to give me courage every time my mother's name is spoken. Her father's name. I have often asked myself what name I would give my children, if I ever had children, and I decided, some time ago already, that I would give them exclusively the name Kanapé, with the original *K*, whoever the father is. So that the line will not be broken, but above all so that Innu names are perpetuated, as much as possible. And also to re-establish the traditional matrilineal system of our people. I'll give my children Innu names so that they know their true name as well as the ancient heritage of a traditionally nomadic people, which is also their heritage. Because I'm very aware of what I absolutely have to transmit to them, through my blood. What I call "the resurgence and transfiguration of the Wound of Colonization."

Empathy. An indispensable tool, as you say. I think you're right. So how are we able to live in a society? These days, we see so many people who, as soon as they feel uncomfortable in society, withdraw from groups. In these cases, we might wonder about their reasons for being part of a group (friends, family, work, etc.). Material comfort and all the things (computers, smart phones …) that now furnish our daily lives are undermining the natural empathy that we have as people living together. I have the impression that as we accumulate more and more stuff, human beings are in danger of losing this natural empathy. Does that go against our evolution? I believe that's already pretty clear.

Language can teach us a lot, however. As I told you, there are a lot of very precise words in the Innu language. So, much empathy for beings and things! For one thing, there are no feminine or masculine grammatical genders as there are in French. And to conjugate the verbs, you have to distinguish between "animate" and "inanimate" subjects, because the prefixes and suffixes that are added to the root are different. To distinguish between animate and inanimate subjects you have to know what exists and doesn't exist. What is natural and what is artificial. What comes directly from the environment and what was transformed by the hand of man. Take a stone and a couch, for example: the former is animate and the latter is inanimate. In the sense that the stone is a living thing. For us, the stone is a being of great knowledge. As we all know, it is an element forged by nature millions, if not billions, of years ago. What came before us and survives through time is therefore a carrier of a great memory. For example, the rocks remember Samuel de Champlain sailing up the Saint Lawrence River at the beginning of the seventeenth century, or they tell us in silence about the Wounded Knee Massacre which took place at the end of the nineteenth century on the Lakota Pine Ridge Indian Reservation in South Dakota, United States. You see, even languages know how to talk to human beings. I believe that our languages, which were forged by the territories of our North America, will be able to contribute to making empathy once again part of everyday speech.

The stones of Oka carry the mark of the crisis inside them. Just as the pines do. One day, I would love to go ask them what they think about it. The solution resides in language. If we asked others to translate for us what surrounds them into their language and, in particular, if we knew how to be attentive to what that person answers, already they would no longer be strangers. The dialogue would have begun. We would maybe even be capable of recognizing their inner language. But we would also have to learn the codes of conversation in their language. Since each language has a distinctive way of thinking, there are various ways of thinking and reflecting, both individually and collectively.

The idea that young Québécois and members of the Indigenous communities should start having this kind of correspondence is, I believe, a way to lay the groundwork of our collective future. In that way, the death of Joe Armstrong during the Oka Crisis will not have been in vain, nor that of Corporal Marcel Lemay. We know only too well how to exploit deaths and murders to make sordid tales or epic films. It is urgent for us to learn to embalm our dead, and to do so in the words of our respective languages.

Which takes me back to the malicious column by that writer we were talking about at the very beginning of our exchange of letters. It was about the death of an eleven-year-old girl, Makayla Sault, who had refused chemotherapy to fight her cancer, which led to a deluge of articles on the debate between modern medicine and the traditional medicine of the First Nations. Makayla had chosen to take an "alternative treatment" offered by the Hippocrates

Health Institute, in Florida, and no one really made the distinction. The case of that young Ontario girl should never have been used as a pretext to start that nasty debate. The media exploited her memory to stir up controversy about Indigenous traditions. How many times have I attempted to say it, to make it understood? But it always comes back to that thorny question. That woman took advantage of the opportunity to make those inflammatory comments about our "deadly culture." I thought about little Makayla, and I asked her for forgiveness.

I also firmly believe that literature is essential, that we have to make it live for all the reasons that we've mentioned, that we have to re-establish its true role. To be visionary, to transpose our visions into words, to contribute a poetry to the world, an interpretation of the world. Literature is the art of language, the art of thought. There exists among us an ancient oral literature, but we are losing it bit by bit every day, second by second. Since it isn't written down, unfortunately it isn't considered literature, but it still exists. I need to learn the stories and legends of my people, which contain all kinds of parables to teach us about life in society, about life in general, and that pass along the basic codes and, at the same time, the memory of past lives. What a vehicle the oral tradition is for transmitting all those principles and all those values! That is why we all have to relearn to talk, to discuss, to clearly perceive the other and, in so doing, show true empathy.

You know, it was only in 2014 that I read some of our ancestral stories for the first time. I was asked to write a new one, based on one of those stories and on a play written by children who had reinterpreted the same story in their own way. That led me to write a new story titled "L'Enfant qui m'avait donné des poux" ("The Child Who Gave Me Lice") that was co-published by Possibles Éditions and Exeko in the Indigenous–Québécois collection *Terres de Trickster / Lands of Trickster*.[14] When I became aware of our stories and legends, thanks to the book *La forêt vive* ("The living forest") by Rémi Savard, in which he studies Innu parables,[15] I learned a lot about myself and my personality, which I found different from that of all my Québécois friends. I learned a lot about my cultural traits. I was better able to understand myself and even justify my way of thinking. I finally saw my way of looking at the world through new eyes. I discovered that my perceptions of the universe had in fact been transmitted to me by all the generations of my people that had gone before me. My blood remembers.

Literature is primordial. But we can see how it is being mistreated these days. We see the void that that creates among our contemporaries. However, we know so many individuals in the book world who, just like us, still believe in the power of literature. That's why we're writing to each other! I believe that this book will contribute new avenues for reflection to our world. That is the role of literature.

Sometimes you have a feeling of being simplistic. I often have that sensation myself, except when I speak in public forums, my instinct tells me I should simplify my words, and that seems to defuse tensions. I'm less afraid, because I know that simplicity and patience can save me being nervous about speaking in public. We try so hard to put words to what we want to criticize, comment on, analyze, that we lose the meaning of what is important. And that's what

---

14   Joséphine Bacon, François Gagnon, Cliff Cardinal, Alexis Martin, Catherine Voyer-Léger, Moe Clark, and Natasha Kanapé-Fontaine, *Terres de Trickster / Trickster Otaski / Akin kadipendag Trickster / Kuekuatsheu / Teshakoierónnions / Wiisagejaak / Lands of Trickster* (Montreal: Possibles Éditions, 2014), with illustrations by Pascale Bonenfant.

15   Rémi Savard, *La forêt vive. Récits fondateurs du peuple innu* [The living forest: Founding narratives of the Innu People] (Montréal: Boréal, 2004).

interests me in this life: the meaning of words. I believe that I have an immense need to give a meaning to everything around me. To give life to what is around me.

Read, you're right, you have to read. I've been thinking about that. How to bring literature to young Indigenous people and convince them of its benefits. The knowledge that I have now I got by reading. I have to confess, though, that I learn and retain things better when I see a lecture. But I love to read and I love books. Giving a taste for reading or theatre to children can be very beneficial to them. Once again, it has to be something that is felt. Something that has meaning. To give literature to childhood is to give it a meaning.

In fact, reading each other looks a lot like that democracy that has been dreamed about so much in which everyone speaks in turn and everyone knows how to listen.

I say *iame uenapissish* to you in turn, my friend. *Kuessipan*, as my people say.

Your turn,
Natasha

15

Kuei, Maikaniss,

We humans are odd, are we not? We want to believe that what makes us human is the way we live – the combination of our beliefs, our daily actions, and our social relations that constitute our culture – even though what makes us human is the diversity of our ways of living. We are creators. We create not only the objects that surround us, but also our way of seeing the world. We invent concepts and believe that they are real: our national identities and the value of our money, our gods, and so forth. But even if diversity is part of our nature, very few things shock us as much as someone who doesn't share our beliefs. Maybe that scares us, reminding us that we don't actually know much about our existence, that we live on a tiny planet among billions of others that we'll never see. Our beliefs protect us from uncertainty and distance us from the natural world of which we nonetheless are part: a nature whose implacable rules demand that we will all disappear one day; a nature against which our inventions cannot eternally protect us.

When I read your letters, I realize that our understanding of the world is very different, and I tell myself, "What wealth!" Personally, I would like to see my culture evolve, become suppler, more inclusive, richer. It is not necessary that I share your beliefs to benefit – with you and with others around us – from this wealth of diversity. When you spoke of animals and their teachers, I recalled stories of ancient yogis who learned their postures from observing animals, and that they gave those poses the names of animals. They tried to incarnate their energies and wisdom so that they could live more at ease in their bodies and in the world. Your description of animals made me more conscious of the way that ancient yogis might have perceived the world (though I recognize that we are speaking of distinct traditions and vastly different world views). This is also true of traditional hunters in a number of Indigenous and African cultures, in which intimate and respectful relationships are established with the prey before and after the hunt. Having listened to you, I feel that my understanding of such stories has deepened. I can imagine them more easily in their details. It's a profound experience to travel in the imagination and return with a new perspective on the world. Thank you!

Of course, White people feel less threatened by stories of animals than by those about the suffering of Indigenous people. It seems to me that in general, Whites like seeing historic "American Indians" in a romantic light; at the same time, they dislike and fear contemporary Indigenous people. Even the mythology that Whites fabricated about "American Indians" is a way of erasing their reality, of condemning them to silence. Telling stories can be positive as easily as it can be negative. We can construct a narrative that hides the truth of the other or simplifies it excessively, as in the case of racism – just as we can also use stories to reveal our complexity. Some people say that all art is revolutionary. I don't believe that to be true. The majority of works of art simply repeat what has already been said, sanctioning the existing social order. And the majority of artists speak in the place of others without truly knowing their stories or without listening. Whites often tell stories about "American Indians" in order to confirm what they like to believe, without searching to understand how Indigenous people themselves perceive those stories.

I often feel somewhat stupefied to see to what degree people like watching TV shows in which the characters have beliefs that diverge wildly from their own (as in fantasy or sci-fi series), but that they have no interest at all in the people with different cultures who live alongside them and who could share authentic world views. No doubt we prefer to be comforted by the knowledge that the beliefs in the TV shows aren't real, whereas those of our neighbours seem threatening. They could show us that we are wrong about many things, that much of what we view as important to us, consciously or not, is perhaps untrue.

European fairy tales and even the Bible speak of the existence of fantastic or supernatural beings: elves, ogres, monsters with human forms, whether gigantic or tiny. After a great deal of thought, I began to wonder whether the stories were actually about humans who dressed differently, who didn't speak the same language or who didn't eat the same types of foods. I can easily imagine two groups of people who eye each other from a distance saying, "Those are monsters!" The monster is the other, the people who are different. In one of my preceding letters, I wrote about the Iraqis whom we so intensely dehumanized during the war that we treated those who died as an "unpeople." Today, almost all Muslims are dehumanized in the media and, more generally, in the eyes of the West. This is similar to what we have done with Indigenous people as well as those of African descent. This dehumanization often takes place when there is a conflict over resources. I ask myself if, one day, we will discover that this reaction has a biological basis: the loss of our empathy for others when we desire their resources or fear that they will take ours. There is already scientific evidence that the human brain (at least the brains of those who have been tested) experiences less empathy for those that it excludes from its group. For instance, in former Yugoslavia, people lived peacefully for decades, but, when they began speaking of each other as different ethnic groups and emphasizing their differences, they were more easily able to kill neighbours who didn't belong to the same group as their own.

In Canada, we must realize the degree to which it is easy to distance ourselves from the ethnic groups that we know the least – from Indigenous people, from immigrants, or from those who do not come from our linguistic community (whether francophone, anglophone, or allophone). We then need to speak rationally to find ways that we can draw closer and put an end to our current era of negligence and distrust, so that we can build an authentic peace.

I return therefore to the question that I asked you in my last letter. Why is it so difficult for Whites to consider Indigenous points of view? Why do Whites deny the problems, territorial rights, and even the suffering of Indigenous people? The answer touches on the guilt that Whites have in relationship to Indigenous people, but that they above all do not want to feel, recognize, or accept. This is a long discussion to which I will return in another letter.

Of equal importance is the question of establishing legal precedents. Each time that a Canadian court renders a favourable judgment to return territories to an Indigenous People, it becomes more difficult for other courts to refuse to do the same. This is the principle of common law. White people ask just how far the situation can go, fearing for what will become of Canada (or the Americas) if we publicly acknowledge how much land we have stolen from Indigenous Peoples. And if we must return territories, when would we stop doing so? Personally, I don't believe that the country would fall apart, but it seems clear to me that the system we currently have would change. I do hope that this happens. Whites have benefitted from the situation; it's time to learn to share the territory more equitably and to recognize that Indigenous values are grounded in a world view that we all need to respect if we're going to inhabit the same country.

We've wandered a good deal into ideas in our recent letters. But while considering these questions rationally, I have been reminding myself of how important it is to foster empathy through stories. Therefore, I have more questions for you. When did you realize that you were Indigenous? How did that happen? How old were you? How did it affect you to realize that you belonged to a group that was marginal in the larger society? How did that change your perceptions at that time?

So … *kuessipan*. What a beautiful word! I will try to say it out loud.

Kuessipan!
Deni

P.S. What is the meaning of the word I just wrote?

16

My dear Deni,

We are back again for our appointment with open dialogue.

I've been thinking and I wonder why we came to this. I wonder why, until now, it has been so difficult for Québécois and Indigenous people to talk openly. Maybe, without the Oka Crisis, without the poisonous words spread by the media, without that racist propaganda that circulated at the time, it would have been less difficult. When I think about the Oka Crisis (I've already said I'm obsessed with it), I feel a crisis erupts inside me, in the sense that I get very upset. Some of us are carrying pain, Deni, my friend: even in our time, we're haunted by the landscapes of yesteryear. We measure the divide between time and us. I call it the Wound of Colonization.

I confess that sometimes I'm afraid I'm idealizing us. Afraid of inventing stories for myself. Of embellishing them. Of transforming what we were into something too beautiful and perfect. I believe that what is haunting us is being adorned with beautiful jewels like pearls of water or moonstones. We're fixated, and we're always feeling a little more regret. Or maybe it's simply that with the shock of concrete, cities, and outfitters, we're telling ourselves that it was good back in the time when we were free.

You know, the word *freedom* doesn't exist in our language. Once I was trying to translate it, and no word came to mind. I was in a car with Joséphine Bacon, an Innu friend writer.[16] We were coming back from an evening in Sainte-Adèle, northwest of Montreal, and returning to the big city. So I asked her the question. She answered that the closest expression was "I am master of myself" or "I govern myself": *nitipenimitishun*. The concept of freedom did not exist before colonization. Then I understood that freedom is primarily in the mind. Freedom comes with knowledge. Knowledge as in knowing about things: beings, things, the world, cultures, mentalities, societies.

Speaking of knowledge, I could talk to you about the knowledge that one can have of oneself. I remember that day, during my adolescence, when I asked myself why I was rather isolated in high school. I was going to my physical education class. Like so many times before, I was feeling melancholy. I don't know what motivated me to ask myself that profound question, to ask myself why I had been marginalized by the other students for many years and also why they weren't more interested in me. I was heading to my class, going into the gym to join my classmates on the bench, when a game of floor hockey had just started. I had stopped playing with the other girls because they thought I played too rough! (I'm laughing as I write down those memories, which are coming back to me more clearly than ever.) And I felt dizzy when my mind finally came up with the conclusion: I was "Amerindian." At that moment, the ground opened up under my feet because I realized that for some time I had been burying that information deep below

---

16   Some of Joséphine Bacon's poetry books were written and published in two languages, Innu-aimun and French. English translations that include the Innu-aimun text are: *Message Sticks / Tshissinuashitakana*, trans. Phyllis Aronoff (Toronto: TSAR Publications, 2013); *A Tea in the Tundra / Nipishapui Nete Mushuat*, trans. Donald Winkler, Canadian Aboriginal Voices series (Markham, Ontario: BookLand Press, 2017).

my consciousness and, above all, because I finally understood that I was experiencing a kind of racism. After that,
I started playing even rougher with the boys during games.

I was being marginalized. All of a sudden I was meas-
uring the cultural traits that separated me from others,
even though we were all young people not very different from one another. I also noticed that every time new
Innu students appeared in a class, in my high school in
Baie-Comeau (located in Quebec's North Shore region,
northeast of Montreal), that they didn't stay very long. And
I would again find myself alone with the other teenagers
of my generation.

Since then, those thoughts have never left me. You
can see how far that has taken me: today, I'm writing you
this letter! In the months that followed my awakening,
I also realized that I was no longer speaking Innu-aimun.
However, I realized, to my surprise, that I still understood
it when it was spoken in front of me! From that moment
on, my ears opened up even more. Innu-aimun: Deni, do
you know how I hear it literally, in my ears? "The speech of
man." If you take *aimun* in isolation, it would maybe be the
Innu word for "speech." Man speaks: it's a miracle, it's a gift.

I'm rediscovering my past by talking to you about people
and my adolescence. After my awakening, I also felt a
great divide between the other Innuat and myself. As if
they were strangers. As if my identity was not the same as
theirs. Self-reflection is an extraordinary journey. I write
books to try to break down a little the consequences of
colonization. Especially those that affect me.

Then came the moment when I discovered the documentary *The Invisible Nation* on television. And my great
adventure began. That was in 2007. The following year,
I decided to go on stage for the first time in my life. Even
though I had been very, very, very silent during my whole

time in high school, I developed an insane desire to sing the way I'd been doing in my room for years. I knew records by heart, whole albums by artists such as Céline Dion – did you know she's a classic in Indigenous communities in Quebec?! – and by the Cirque du Soleil. I listened to RockDétente radio (nowadays called Rouge FM) in the evening, with all those ballads, and, last but not least, to Innu singer-songwriter Florent Vollant. It was odd that he was the only Innu in my parents' record collection, but I adopted him unconsciously, until I knew all the words of his songs by heart simply because I understood Innu-aimun … And then one evening, I told my mother I wanted to take part in the year-end show at school. She suggested I sing one of Florent's songs. It had never occurred to me to do that. I had no idea what an inner storm that plan would throw me into. I had guides, the people who organized the show and who asked me the right questions about my relationship to the song I had chosen, "Miam Maikan," which means: "(I feel) like the wolf." My relationship with my mother tongue, with my identity. I didn't know yet who I was as a person and I didn't know either who I was as an Innu. In hindsight, I can say that those events were actually just the first strange phases of what would follow and that have contributed to what I've become today.

A few years later, I managed to make the leap to the other side of the Saint Lawrence River to study in Rimouski, a larger town in Quebec's Bas-Saint-Laurent region, in order to get out of the reserve, away from the North Shore, and give myself a chance to start afresh. But before that I have to talk to you about my return to the Pessamit Innu Reserve. I spent eight months there in 2010. At that time, I couldn't stand the city anymore and I never once left the reserve during the eight months I spent there. I didn't want to leave as long as I hadn't found what had brought me back there.

You know, in the month of August, just when I was leaving to Rimouski for my studies in visual arts, I had still not found inner peace. I was asking myself questions. I still didn't feel Innu enough to believe that speaking my mother tongue again would be enough for me.

It happened a little before I left. Someone I ran into in a store in the village suddenly said this to me, without warning: "You know you don't need to speak your language to be innushkuess [an Innu girl]! It doesn't matter if you don't speak it! You are Innu inside, and that's enough to be you. I recognize you."

I left a few days later, very quickly, for Rimouski.

I had found my answer.

I needed to know what would come next.

I was looking for a sense of belonging.

Niaut nuitsheuakan,
Natasha

P.S. *Kuessipan* means "to you!" It's your turn. In a game, or in a conversation, or when, with Joséphine Bacon, we give a joint reading, there is always that moment when she finishes her poem, then she whispers to me very softly on stage: "Kuessipan." Sometimes, among us, we also say "tshin," which means "you." That's what I say most often. But in the case of our exchange of letters, *kuessipan* is the best term to use to tell the other person that it's their turn.

Kuessipan, nuitsheuakan.

17

Good evening, Maikaniss,

How do we say "good evening" in Innu-aimun?

I truly appreciated your reflection on the word *freedom*. How many non-Indigenous people know that they have lived so close to a people for whom the notion of freedom does not concern the relationship we have with others, but with ourselves? Achieving freedom by mastering oneself: to me, this sounds similar to the path of the Buddha, even if I am well aware that you are speaking of a philosophy that is entirely distinct, with its own wealth of history and subtleties.

Nitipenimitishun: "I am the master of myself."

I am trying to imagine what our relationship with nature will become and how much freer we will be if we arrive at knowing ourselves. When I say "know oneself," I am speaking of the experience of self-knowledge in the world. If we surround ourselves with people who resemble us, we reduce the world in which we live and we drastically limit what we can become. But if we do not close ourselves off and if we open ourselves to the world – a world that isn't reduced to our own reflection – we can better understand the immensity of human potential. Maybe when we arrive at mastering our reactions to fear and discomfort, the world will open itself to us. But this is where my imagination reaches its limits, since I am considering Innu philosophy through the lens of the philosophies that I already know, when it could in truth be totally different from all that I could have considered until recently. Despite that, I can imagine that if the encounter between Indigenous and European cultures had been more peaceful, thousands of people would today take the path of Nitipenimitishun, just as thousands travel to India and to Asian countries to study the teachings of the Hindus and Buddhists.

In your last letter, the section in which you describe your growing awareness of your Indigenous identity was, for me, equally thought-provoking. I asked myself if Whites experienced similar moments or if their sense of belonging to a majority culture is so strong that they never truly become aware of it. Surely there are Whites who realize and others who never ask themselves this question. This reminds me of White children who entertain themselves by saying: "I could have been born (insert here the word designating what they are not, such as 'in a poor country' or 'a member of an ethnic group that isn't White or privileged')." This game is no doubt linked to their parents who say: "Eat your food. You could have been born in Africa, you know. You're lucky." As a child, I considered what I was not, even though I wasn't yet aware of what I was – that I was White. And yet I was conscious of all that I wasn't as well as what I was "lucky" (according to adults) not to be.

For the past several years, I have thought a great deal about invisible privilege. It's an idea that I now often hear mentioned in discussions about racism (and feminism as well). One day, after having spent the week writing about this subject, I ran across a TED Talk online. Michael Kimmel, an American sociologist, was speaking about an African American friend who, when she looked in the mirror, saw a "Black" woman, and about a White friend who, when she looked in the mirror, saw a woman. He explained that when he looked in the mirror, he saw a human being. He shares how he realized that, unconsciously, he thought of himself as "the generic person," as if his experience of life had something universal about it. The African American woman was aware of her difference in relationship to the social norm (the "White man"). She knew that she was a woman and that she was African American, whereas the White woman saw herself more or less as a generic woman. Kimmel, however, simply perceived himself as human. He didn't actively view himself as a White man, because White men are at the epicentre of power, looking outward at those at the margins; they are the ones who put labels on all of those who are not like them and whom, historically, they have excluded from power. Kimmel emphasized how privilege is invisible for those who hold it and how Whites have the luxury of not having to think about questions of race every second of their lives. I was startled hearing him speak, since I'd had exactly that expression in my head all week: invisible privilege. I'd been asking myself in my writings how it was possible to make this reality visible to Whites, how to oblige them to perceive the privilege that they hold: how their lives are easier, how their ideas dominate the world, and how those who aren't White – or White men, in particular – struggle to make a place for themselves and be heard.[17]

What Kimmel addresses is one of the central problems of racism. Whites see themselves as the norm. They ask fewer questions about their existence and their worth. Personally, I had to learn to listen to other points of view, since at times I wasn't aware that others weren't receiving

---

17   See Michael Kimmel, "Why Gender Equality is Good for Everyone – Men Included," filmed May 2015 in Monterey, CA, TED Talk, 15:58, https://www.ted.com/talks/michael_kimmel_why_gender_equality_is_good_for_every one_men_included.

the same privileges that I was. Even if I grew up poor and with challenges, the simple fact of being a White man certainly helped me achieve my ambitions. When I was young, I saw above all what I didn't have, without realizing that others had much less and that society offered them far fewer chances simply because of their appearance.

I have since spent a good deal of time observing interactions between people. White men are far more at ease asking for what they want and saying what they think, as if everyone should listen to them. White women hesitate a little more but, in general, they appear – to my eye at least – more at ease than many ethnic minorities.

I wish that Whites could take a moment to observe the daily experiences of numerous minorities and to see how different those experiences are. Of course, certain people are resilient and achieve their goals despite the coldness of White society. But I have tried to take the time to see how people from other ethnic groups are treated in public places, whether in restaurants, in banks, or even in convenience stores. Others are often much less warm with them, or simply openly rude. For minorities, I can only imagine the ways that this can be tiring or discouraging. However, in my contact with them, they generally complain far less than White people, perhaps because they don't expect to receive everything with relative ease. They don't necessarily go about life expecting everyone to listen to their problems. They have known injustice, or indifference, and they aren't surprised, the way Whites can be, when life doesn't turn out in their favour. Speaking of complaining, how many times have I heard Whites in Quebec or the United States say that minorities profit from the system, that African Americans receive too many scholarships, that Indigenous people have too much given to them by the government. Whites speak of their difficulties, but they don't seem to realize to what degree society is turned against those who aren't White. White society enjoys perpetual handouts and subsidies.

Those who are in power often think that their way of seeing the world is fair, and they are afraid of losing power and privileges. Few people are aware that their reactions are above all visceral while the reasoning with which they justify racism is cerebral and doesn't take into consideration the underlying fears that motivate them. They often affirm that "_____" people are lazy and that they want everything for free, that they don't work hard like White people. In reality, good jobs are often not open to people from minority groups and this alone can be profoundly discouraging. Or rather many of them work harder than many White people, but doing jobs that White people don't want.

I've seen this situation in different contexts around the world. Growing up, I heard numerous English Canadians say similar things about the Québécois, especially when anglophones were angry about political demands in Quebec. But everything of which they accused the Québécois was but a fraction of what English Canadians had themselves done for centuries in order to maintain power. It is never pleasant to realize that a system that doesn't directly benefit us is being put in place. The Québécois have perceived themselves as the victims of the anglophones, as those who survived a racist system that was turned against them. They still maintain this discourse, even if, since then, their lives have improved. As for many, when the system benefits us, we cease to be aware of it. As I wrote in a preceding letter, we take it for granted; to our eyes, it becomes invisible.

How can we use our imaginations and empathy to help people see the degree to which the experiences of others can be different from our own? Take for example the 1970 October Crisis in Quebec: nearly five hundred people were arrested without respect to their civil rights, after the government invoked the War Measures Act.[18] How do we explain the arrests? Knowing that the five hundred people they arrested knew thousands of others, the authorities likely wanted to bring fear into the communities sympathetic to the Front de libération du Québec. The intimidation resembles that used for decades by many Canadian police against Indigenous people, or by American police toward African American people.

In his book *Just Mercy*, the author, lawyer, and African American activist Bryan Stevenson describes a moment when two police stopped and searched him without respecting his rights.[19] Stevenson had done nothing illegal, but the police pointed their firearms at him and, even though he was a lawyer and had a strong understanding of police and legal protocol (not to mention his rights), he was so afraid that he almost ran away to save himself. It was then that he realized how fear could cause so many young African American people to react poorly in front of police and be killed. In 2017 alone, 220 African American people were killed by police, and the increasing publicization of those deaths has revealed to many the violence against African American communities.[20]

---

18   The October Crisis (in French, "la crise d'Octobre") primarily took place in Montreal when the separatist group Le Front de libération du Québec ("Quebec Liberation Front"), or "FLQ," kidnapped the provincial Minister of Labour Pierre Laporte and the British diplomat James Cross. Canadian Prime Minister Pierre Trudeau invoked the War Measures Act – the only time in Canada's history that it was used during peace time. The members of the FLQ murdered Laporte and, after a period of negotiations, released Cross, before going into exile in Cuba.

19   Bryan Stevenson, "Stand," chapter 2 in *Just Mercy: A Story of Justice and Redemption* (New York: Spiegel & Grau, 2014).

20   "Unarmed black people were killed by police at 5x the rate of unarmed whites in 2015." Quoted from "2015 Unarmed Victims," Mapping Police Violence, accessed December 2017, http://mappingpoliceviolence.org/unarmed/.

In Quebec, the Indigenous women who have been victims of police aggression in and around the city of Val-d'Or, in Quebec's Abitibi-Témiscamingue region, reveal the degree to which the problem of police violence remains serious and constant. Eight officers with the Sûreté du Québec, Quebec's Provincial Police, were suspected of having used their power to intimidate Indigenous women and sexually abuse them. I often hear Whites discussing similar situations without appearing bothered and I have asked them what their reaction would be if eight Indigenous men had been raping White women. In general, their reaction changes completely. For the majority of Whites, it is difficult to imagine a world in which the police appear a predatory force that targets minorities and vulnerable groups simply because such behaviour is tolerated. A few years ago, I was speaking with a White woman about a White American man who lived in the Democratic Republic of the Congo and who, according to several sources, frequently slept with underage African girls. The woman told me that such things took place often in Africa, as if this was no problem. I then asked her how she would react if a sexual predator was doing the same thing in an American city, and she immediately responded that the situation would be different, that it wouldn't be acceptable.

Victims of these sorts of stories can be found everywhere, but many are afraid to speak out, since those who are supposed to protect them are often the same people who abuse them. How can they trust a system that inflicts this sort of violence on their bodies? The irony is that many White people speak of their fear of minorities, but they fail to consider that minorities are the people who are truly living in fear and who are most often in danger.

I would like to return to the subject of trauma. I have noticed that small traumas experienced by members of my family or by friends have prevented them from having the lives that they want. I wish that the Québécois or other previously marginalized White groups, such as the Irish, would consider the historical repression of which they have been victim and imagine the situations thousands of times worse that other minorities had to endure – and then admit that this type of ostracism exists today. How can people be part of a society when its system is designed to exclude them, when they know that the majority dislikes them, when they simply aren't welcome? Whites can respond that members of other ethnic groups are welcome if they integrate into society, but this isn't true. Invisible privilege allows Whites to speak in this way.

Often, when Whites speak of past suffering, we say, "I survived. Now I'm doing well. Why can't others achieve everything I have?" I've heard this many times. But we say this while thinking only about our own challenges. We don't recognize all of the support that society has given us, how much we benefitted in ways that others haven't, and were protected in ways that others weren't. The majority of Whites have interiorized from a young age that they are superior, and what happens to them in life seems significantly more important than what happens to other people. There are historic reasons to explain this and I will return to them in a later letter. But where is the compassion if we don't look at our own suffering to better understand the greater intensity of that experienced by others? Where are we headed as a society?

James Baldwin, the African American writer and social critic, wrote that White men "believe the world is theirs and [...], albeit unconsciously, expect the world to help them in the achievement of their identity." But he adds that the universe doesn't do this for anyone. It isn't interested in our identity. Baldwin adds that "the anguish which can overtake a white man comes in the middle of his life," the moment when he has to reconsider not only his beliefs and expectations, but his entire identity – the moment when he enters into the unknown.[21] This seems accurate to me. It is almost inevitable that we will one day realize that we are less special than we previously believed.

Among White communities, there are creative and generous cultures, but we often remain blind to our failures. We have evolved a great deal over the last century and I hope that we will continue to do so. Now is the time to show humility rather than to perpetuate the suffering that arises from an ethnocentric mythology that harms all of humanity.

What is Innu culture like? What did you experience when you returned to live on the reservation? I would like to have a better understanding of that experience.

Iame uenapissish,
Deni

---

21   James Baldwin, *Nobody Knows My Name* (New York: Vintage Books, 1961), 189.

18

Kuei, kuei, Deni,

To think about the word *freedom* is to think about humanity.

To answer another of your questions, the phrase *good evening* doesn't seem to exist in our language, to my (limited) knowledge. There's always the greeting *Kuei*, but another way to greet someone that we care about, a friend or a family member, is to make jokes to announce our arrival. And to have a good laugh.

Innu means "human being." I believe that I was so frightened by the loss of my mother tongue that now I take advantage of every way possible to learn it.

I'm realizing for the first time how much my childhood is tied up with Innu-aimun. Why did I so rarely dip into those memories that the Montreal autumn suddenly brought back to the surface? I try to retrieve from my memory those first years of my life when everything, absolutely everything, happened in Innu-aimun. There was only my small town of Pessamit. The snow. The houses of my paternal and maternal grandparents. The smell of the game inside. The songs of my paternal grandfather who beat the rhythm with his fist on the table. The name of the animals in our language. The smell of the woods and the outdoors on the coats of my maternal grandfather.

I have often tried to imagine the person I would have become if my parents had stayed on the reserve and I had grown up there. I wonder if I feel so strongly about claiming my identity as an innushkueu (Innu woman) and if I would have been so proud to be an Indigenous woman as I am today. In recent years, I have read in the social media that young Indigenous people have gained awareness of this difference in levels of identity affirmation. I've also had many conversations on the subject with other people of my generation during my stays on the reserve. There, at home, we don't feel the need to assert loud and clear that we are Innu for the simple reason that we are surrounded by Innuat. Outside the reserve is where things change. We find ourselves facing adversity. We are confronted by the other. Someone else who is in a dominant position. Who is everywhere.

You know, those others I'm talking about are seen as being dominant. They came in big wooden boats, they came with their machines, they came to build hydroelectric dams. They came with their forestry companies, with their mining companies, with their factories. They are still searching, searching for uranium, searching for oil, searching for sand. They came and soiled everything, turned everything upside down, smashed everything. Since their arrival, the ancestral territory has been defiled. The territory is being smothered.

Unless the system is toppled, unless those machines are turned off, there's not much we can do. No one, not even that other one. I'd like to add that, in spite of everything and whatever happens, those others are also the ones who came with their knowledge, with their literature, their writing, their new language, their prayers, their conviction, and their fascination with the country. They came with their books. They came with their poetry. I'm not saying we didn't have those things, I'm saying that you came with riches that fed ours.

I've travelled quite a bit thanks to poetry, which has allowed me to encounter many different cultures and several new languages. All those cultures have helped to shape how I see the world and, especially, how I define myself as a young Innu woman in the world. I'm aware that young people today are experiencing the encounter with the other differently, in particular in this era of social networks. All the same young Indigenous people still too often run into walls when they land in the city: the society, the language, the social codes, the material references.

What about going back? Returning to the reserve? I have the impression that so many years have gone by since I did that! It's been barely five years though. It was in January 2010, shortly after the death of singer Lhasa de Sela, which really affected me. I decided to go back and live at home. Why? In the fall, after a summer spent in Pessamit, I tried a return to the city, but I didn't find work or funding to continue my studies (I hadn't passed my courses the year before). My failure was both financial and moral. So I started to drink, though I'd never really consumed alcohol before. Alcohol became my only escape. I'd go out every weekend. All my money went to that. I stopped paying my rent, I ignored my electricity bills, I barely ate. The end of 2009 was not very restful and I spent the first week of January 2010 in Baie-Comeau in a community for alcoholics. One evening, I went to the religious community that, in a way, had raised me as a child and adolescent. I wanted to see familiar faces again, but I realized at that moment that my place was no longer in the city, that I was looking for something else. I remember, during a return trip to Pessamit a few weeks earlier, that I had had premonitions that I'd go back there. My body was calling for its childhood village the way a child cries for her mother's breast.

Inside myself it was far from easy. I thought I was pale-skinned, so White. I was almost ashamed to speak French, because it wasn't part of my ideal (there are still days like that, you know). I thought in French. And yet, I'm not Métis. Both my parents are native to the village. Everyone knows them, at least by name. Or if not them, my grandparents. In the village, people sometimes ask you who you are, and specifically who your parents are if you are of a certain generation.

I reconnected with the families of both my parents. I didn't really know them, even though I had met them when I was a child. I ended up babysitting my cousins' children in order to have the kind of family life that I'd never known when I lived in the city. Then I started working in the little store at the entrance to the village. It was one of the best ways I'd found to be recognized. For months, people asked me who I was, where I came from, who my parents were. By hearing Innu-aimun on a daily basis, it finally got into my head again. I relearned the language by analyzing the way people talked and thought. I listened to their words as much as their silences. And sometimes, the silences are much more meaningful than the words themselves.

I didn't stay for a long time on the reserve. I finally went back to school. I wanted to go back to Pessamit every summer, though, but I ended up not going, looking at the poverty there with my city eyes, a poverty combined with the laughter and resilience of a people that has been able to survive. That's also what attracts me there, what makes it different from the city: mutual aid, the sharing of material and immaterial things, enjoying the good things in life, living in spite of all the "in spite ofs" and trusting in tomorrow, even though tomorrow is always another day. A slow, quiet, cyclical life perhaps, out of step with the outside world, where everything goes too fast, at breakneck speed, and that sucks in everyone who dares to venture there. You have to row against the current, if you want to stay there. If not, you come back to the village like castaways. How many times have I dreamed of returning there to sit down on the verandas and watch other people going by on the street, with their children, their strollers, their new lovers, their exes? Watch the elders roll by in electric wheelchairs in high gear, even though that speed actually matches their walking pace when they were healthy.

There is still a great danger: that the collective amnesia that was deliberately created by past governments will finally crush my generation. That the only individuals left won't know why they're here, won't know anymore that the true Innu culture is the old words of the language of the territory. And that's what scares me. The most spiritual people in the community are looked at as being a little bizarre, a little lost in their imaginings. As if their sensitivity to the environment was a superficial, insignificant thing. As if that relationship with nature hadn't been forged by our ancient societies, century after century.

I don't know, Deni. Looking back on that part of my life brings me back to my sadness and my disappointment with leading a life detached from our precolonial past. There are days when I feel like getting up and taking the "road home" on Route 138, which starts at the end of Sherbrooke Street East, here, in Montreal. I'd go establish a new system that would liberate my village from the dominant society and its consumption mentality. I'd bring down the chiefs and I'd revive agriculture. I'd mobilize human resources from the outside to train our people (and those resources would afterward have the wisdom to leave in order for us to be autonomous). I'd give back the money to the people; I'd create vegetable gardens and install solar panels; I'd divide up the territory of the reserve into family lots; I'd get the forestry companies out; I'd preach that colonialism is what is destroying us, that it's the White world that is asphyxiating us, that we have to recreate our own world and go back to our roots that are dying among the tree trunks that have fallen on the ground of the reserve. I'd become chief, if only to restore our traditional democracy. I'm fed up. I'm smothering among the buildings of the city. I suffer every day from not drinking the water of the rivers of the North. I suffer every day from knowing that toxic waters are dumped on the body of the Mushuau, "the land without trees," today called Labrador.

I suffer every day. Sometimes I put aside those dark ideas and I go on with my life. We mustn't idealize our past. Nor our future lives. All the more so given that we are in the grip of a world that is slowly falling apart. How can we hope to survive that if we're the most disadvantaged people? Surely by attempting to bring a little light to it, as I want to do for my generation ... And yet I believe firmly that, when this world in which we have so much trouble surviving collapses of its own accord, we'll feel a lot better. We'll perhaps be able to again become what we are. We'll rebuild ourselves, day by day.

Many things still disturb me and this look back at my memories brings back my repressed anger. I see my journey again and I see that my current situation is not very different from those times when I had lost my way. I therefore feel resentful about history and colonization, even though I'm well aware that that's not the thing to do. I thought I was better, that I'd been able to find balance in my life, but now recent events have again forced me to fight for what I desire. Everything is transformed into an inner, superhuman struggle to achieve grace. All that is simply human, after all.

If we want to believe we can change the world, we have to first and foremost know how to *be*.

Hugs, Deni,
Natasha

19

Kuei, nuitsheuakan,

What a journey you've made! I hope you are proud of your-self. I felt in your words how much you have suffered but also how much worth you give to what you have attained – that your wisdom comes not only from books but also from the complexity of your life.

Reading your letter, I imagined myself in your place, trying to build a relationship with my people, to situate myself within a majority society that constantly reminds me that there is something wrong with what I am. I can only begin to imagine how much you must have had to search within yourself to find the strength to confront that reality.

I also saw your experiences through the lens of my own life. When I was young, I learned that it was shameful to be Québécois. My father often told me that the Québécois were backward, that they were poor and violent, dominated by priests and alcoholism. The image that he evoked for me came from the memories of his childhood: the abuses of the parish priest in his village in Gaspésie, the authority of the Catholic Church, the hardships of daily life, the poverty before the Quiet Revolution,[22] the lack of education and

22   The Quiet Revolution (in French, "la Révolution tranquille") was a period in Quebec's history during which political and cultural change led to the creation of secular society (after centuries of the Catholic Church's rule) as well as to the rise of the sovereigntist movement.

opportunities. He would tell my mother that my sister, my brother, and I shouldn't learn French, since he thought it served no purpose. He didn't want us to come across as francophones, since that could create hardship for us and make us feel marginalized.

I have a clear sense of where those impulses came from in him. He broke off his relationship with his family in Quebec and almost never spoke of them, not even mentioning their names. But my mother insisted that I learn French. So I went to an immersion program, where many of my friends were the children of other Québécois living in British Columbia. When I was ten, we moved to the United States, and my mother made me spend time with a Belgian family as well as take French classes so that I wouldn't lose the language.

Ten years later, shortly after I turned twenty and just before my father's death, he told me his real name, my grandmother's name, as well as where she lived in Quebec – in a town called Matane, on the northern side of the Gaspé Peninsula. Later, when he was deceased, I made the trip to Gaspésie to meet my family and lived several years in Quebec to gain a better sense of my roots. I found it difficult to understand my place within the two cultures – if not three cultures – I had grown up in, since I'd lived in the United States, in English Canada, and in Quebec. Even though many aspects of the culture of my Québécois family, and of Quebec in general, were familiar, I was raised with a great deal of freedom, often in poverty, and, with my rather nomadic way of life, never had to be accountable to anyone. The situation was in some ways similar to that which you described: I found many social codes difficult to integrate into my life, though I can imagine that the experience was far less severe than the one you described.

Recently, I wrote an article about the Québécois roots

of the American novelist and poet Jack Kerouac.[23] He grew up in a francophone community in Massachusetts at a time when racism against French Canadian immigrants was extremely present, since hundreds of thousands of largely impoverished people from Quebec had migrated to New England and established communities in its industrial centres. American newspapers ran articles claiming that the French Canadians were a menace for American society and compared them to Indigenous people in their refusal to assimilate to the majority culture. Anglophones used pejorative words to designate francophones, calling them "frogs" or even "white niggers."[24] Thousands of French Canadians changed their names so that their children wouldn't be harassed in school. Kerouac did the same. Born Jean-Louis Kérouac, he published his first book as John Kerouac and his second as Jack Kerouac ("Jack" having an even more American resonance than "John").

Though French was his maternal language, he wrote several texts in French in which he said that he no longer had a language of his own. He emphasized that he felt lost between the two languages, English and French, and he spoke of his frustration with trying to become American. At the same time, he often hid his French Canadian identity so that he could appear more American. Maybe he'd realized that Americans didn't want to read books written

---

23   "On le Road," *The Walrus*, illustrations by Iveta Karpathyova, November 17, 2016, accessed January 2017, https://thewalrus.ca/on-le-road/; see also Deni Ellis Béchard, "Jack Kerouac," in *Legacy: How French Canadians Shaped North America*, ed. André Pratte and Jonathan Kay (Toronto: Signal, 2016), 297.

24   It is important to point out that even though this epithet was used against Québécois immigrants, the appropriation of the racist term to designate them in no way indicates an experience analogous to the trauma, discrimination, disenfranchisement, dehumanization, and systemic oppression experienced by Americans of African descent.

by a Québécois. But in several of his notebooks and novels, he wrote that he felt torn between his two identities and that he dreamed of returning to live in Quebec.

I am telling this story because I hope that the Québécois, as well as other White people from various ethnic groups, can understand that the cultural oppression they inflict on Indigenous people is worse than that which they themselves have experienced. If we can succeed in seeing how much oppression has harmed our own people, perhaps it is easier to understand its effect on other groups.

When I was young, I could neither see this oppression nor understand how violent it can feel to be constantly reminded by society that we don't fit what is presented as the norm. This violence, like privilege, is generally invisible for those who conform to the mainstream. In fact, those who identify with the norm often see people who are different as threats. They perceive difference as an act of aggression, even violence, even if it is not. People who belong to the dominant culture don't understand the degree to which the system is more powerful than minority groups. It's for that reason that the point of view of marginalized people is so important for a balanced society: they often see more clearly the defining traits of the dominant culture.

But who among us truly listens to minority voices? I used to think that I listened to them. All that I read about Indigenous people was very romantic: an Edenic mythology constructed by White people to emphasize how far we have strayed from nature and how much we have destroyed it. Nostalgic stories of the noble "Indians" of the Great Plains, created for White audiences, hid the suffering of Indigenous people.

I first became aware of this suffering when I was fifteen. I had just returned to live in British Columbia with my father, after a five-year period during which I hadn't seen him. I'd enrolled in a secondary school in the suburbs of Vancouver and, one day, when I was walking down a street with my friends, I saw a girl my age waiting in a car and told my friends that she was pretty. They looked at her and began to laugh. "She's a Paiute," one of them told me. "Paiutes aren't pretty." I asked what a Paiute was, since I'd never heard the word before. In reality, it refers to a First Nations group that doesn't even live in British Columbia, but racists there use the word to refer to Indigenous people in general. The girl had dark hair, but, at our school, there were young people from numerous ethnic groups who had dark hair. To my untrained eye, she could have belonged to many of those different communities. The boys I was with made fun of me, laughing, even though I still didn't understand. They spoke as if what they were saying was obvious, as if what I'd said was impossible.

I thought about this experience for a long time and, little by little, I understood that between the myths surrounding Indigenous people and the racism of my friends, there was another reality of which I knew nothing. I also understood that the life of the girl in the car would probably be difficult, since many people would judge her simply on the basis of her appearance, without even speaking to her. I found myself wondering what her experience of creating a place in the world would be like.

At that time I had already understood – at least superficially – the racism toward African American people in the United States. I encountered it when I was ten, during my first day at school in Virginia. The other White students in my class explained to me why I shouldn't be friends with "black kids." Later, after an African American girl spoke with me, several White boys I knew pretended to vomit. I was afraid to speak with her afterward. Living in Vancouver years later, I had similar experiences when other kids my age talked about immigrants.

As children, often without realizing it, we learn to look down on people who are different. We learn to do this by listening to the views that White adults hold of these people, and by never listening to the people themselves. Jokes are one way of speaking in place of another group and of denying their worth. They also give the people who repeat them a justification for ignoring and disrespecting the human beings they concern. I realized the power of jokes when I was eighteen, living in New England. People there still told jokes in which French Canadians were portrayed as stupid. I began to realize how easy it is, simply by repeating jokes about those with whom we have little or no genuine contact, to end up believing in unfair and cruel depictions.

It took me years to untangle everything I learned about racism, to realize that we imprison people in caricatures. We invent grotesque masks that we oblige others to wear. And the only information that we have about those people comes, in general, from what White people say about them among themselves. Even when we meet them in our daily lives, we don't see people who share many of the same experiences in life; we have so fully dehumanized them that we are no longer able to see them as complete human beings.

The Montreal-born novelist Saul Bellow, who won the 1976 Nobel Prize for Literature, evokes in one of his novels how any form of suppression or repression holds everyone back and affects all of us negatively: "There is no fineness or accuracy of suppression; if you hold down one thing you hold down the adjoining."[25] Earlier, I spoke of the

---

25   Saul Bellow, *The Adventures of Augie March* (New York: Viking Press, 1953), 3.

freedom of forging our own identity, but do we really have that freedom? What would we be today if we grew up in a culture without racism? We would certainly have more freedom to explore difference. We would be more open to other cultures, more connected to the creativity that often arises when cultures come together. We would have access to types of identities of which we might not otherwise be able to conceive.

Like me, you have lived between two cultures and I imagine that, likewise, the language that you master doesn't always feel like your true one, while that which you know less well contains elements crucial to your identity.

You already spoke about freedom, about "Nitipenim-itishun" – "I am master of myself" – and I wonder what freedom means to you today. Do you think that you understand it differently from the majority of non-Indigenous people?

Kuessipan!
Deni

20

Kuei, my dear Deni,

I've taken a few days to answer you. Today I'm writing to you to tell you how grateful I am. Discussing these things with you enables me to take my own reflections further regarding the relationships between peoples and cultures, between languages. I want to thank you right away, even though I don't really know what will finally come of this epistolary adventure! But talking, talking with you does me a lot of good. I never would have imagined that such a dialogue were possible.

Suddenly, though, I have a feeling I'm fooling myself. We're writing each other letters thinking that no one has been able to exchange such words, but how many extra-ordinary individuals have already found ways to initiate discussion on the painful subject of racism?

I wonder. In fact, I'm searching for the path that will lead me to facing up to myself, facing my feelings, facing my own racism. Because I am a racist! I realize that. I work in this society, I speak against racism, I want to uproot the giant tree of settler society, of colonialism, but I don't know how to face my own racism! Maybe I speak this way in order to root it out of me. To convince myself that I'm clean, that I'm right, that I have the right to talk this way, to confront others when I don't do it with myself. Because I have to confess to you, Deni, when I've looked deep inside myself in my latest messages, I've found it very upsetting. I've come face to face with myself! I've stumbled over my racism! I read you, I hear you, I'm happy with our exchange but, deep down, I'm only half-listening to you. Maybe I'm fooling myself again … When we talk to each other, when I broach the subject of racism, I get all fired up! I want to change so radically the foundation of this society that was built on my body, on my being, on my consciousness. Because I identify with my people, with the people that they tried to eradicate – and when they weren't able to kill us, they raped us and deconstructed us.

But now the "me" is coming through in my words again. What is heard is my cry, my person, and not an entire people. Why do I speak as "I" when we are talking about *us*? Why am I driven by the wound? Why am I afraid of myself? Why don't you ask the same questions as I do? When you come face to face with yourself, isn't that the door the light tries to get in through?

Where then is the solution we dream of so ardently? You ask me what freedom means to me. Freedom for me is related to sovereignty. Freedom, in the individual sense, means precisely mastery of oneself. Mastery of one's ideas, reflections, body, feelings, emotions, and spirituality. Mastery of one's sense of sharing, of one's meaning of listening. That's my idea of freedom. I'll always remember the title of a poetry collection by the stunning Syrian poet Maram al-Masri, *Elle va nue la liberté* ("Freedom, she comes naked.").[26] That book was unsettling to me. One morning, recently, I woke up bathed in the sunlight pouring through the window onto my bed, and I quickly got up to make myself some coffee. I was barefoot and I remember the feeling of the wood of the floor under the soles of my feet. I thought

---

26   Maram al-Masri, *Elle va nue la liberté* (Paris: Éditions Bruno Doucey, 2013).

about that title, particularly about the sound of the word *freedom* itself. It reminded me of this poem by Paul Éluard:

> *On health restored*
> *On risk vanished*
> *On hope without memory*
> *I write your name*
>
> *And through the power of a word*
> *I start my life again*
> *I was born to know you*
> *To name you*
>
> *Freedom.*

Titled "Freedom" ("Liberté" in French), this poem was written by Éluard in 1942, during the occupation of France by Hitler's army.[27] Freedom is beautiful, it is wild, it comes from the other, it comes from nature, and it goes naked. It goes naked on the roofs of Beirut, it goes naked on the roofs of Paris, it goes naked on the paths of migrants. Freedom sobs with them, laughs with the homeless in all the cities, sings with all the Nomads of the world. Seeking a refuge for itself, a refuge for identity, a refuge for the inner people. No one can define freedom itself, except if you listen to it, except if you feel it going barefoot on the asphalt.

Where then is the solution we dream of so ardently? An open door for freedom. An open door for identity. An open door for Being. We're looking for solutions, sometimes

---

27   Originally published in the clandestine collection *Poésie et vérité 1942* [Poetry and truth 1942], then after the war in the collection *Au rendez-vous allemand* [literally: At the German appointment] (Paris: Éditions de Minuit, 1945; 2012 edition under the title *Au rendez-vous allemand*, suivi de *Poésie et vérité 1942*, Collection Double).

desperately, but we don't know how to open the door that will take us out of ourselves. What do you dream about, Deni?

I dream of a refuge for racism, because it has itself so much trouble existing that it must need rest. And the racists? Aren't they also trying to understand themselves, but they come face to face with their own inner emptiness, the result of knowledge and awareness not being transmitted? Because we also have to face up to the deficiencies in education in Quebec and in Canada. Almost no one knows anymore how to learn; no one has a desire for learning. And what is taught to students is rote learning, learning by heart, and not with the heart.

Keeping citizens in ignorance alienates them. That also means alienating all the other ethnic, cultural, and spiritual groups that make up society. Everyone who wants to come together to be together, to recognize one another.

It is believed that the solution is reconciliation. Except that reconciliation can itself take many paths. We need to search inside ourselves for the paths that are needed for us to come together. The coming together of the self with the self, the coming together of the self with the other.

Reconciliation calls for reparation. But how many times has reconciliation been deceived? As many times as there have been treaties signed. But what is the use of those treaties if they are only betrayed? What is the use of reconciliation if it is only disappointed?

We are corresponding. Me, in Montreal, and you, during your journeys. We continue along the path of all those who have gone before us on that road of dreamed speech, of neglected speech. We sign each letter like a new treaty but, here, our exchanged words would be difficult to betray. Because we are political and we are real. We are authentic.

We know how to learn, we teach each other. We devote ourselves to knowing.

I'll come back to the question of language. I got carried away talking about freedom.

Freedom has kidnapped me. It has impassioned me. I embrace it.

I embrace you,
Natasha

21

Dear Natasha,

You're right. We're not the first people to write to each other in this way, to try to cross the cultural distance that separates us, and to better understand each other. I imagine that thousands of people have done so before us and I hope that millions of others will take the same path. Without a sincere and concerted effort to improve communication, what can we hope to achieve as a society and as a species?

And what is the point of using writing? Why have we decided to explore this subject with words, without knowing where it would take us? In regards to that question, I have several thoughts.

Writing in this way allows us to cast light on questions that concern our society. In this way, we are participating – as all members of our society should – in an effort to better understand our trajectory, not only as individuals but as a group. Each letter is an invitation to the other, an act of inclusion. We're saying to each other and to all those who read us: "Welcome, we hope that you participate, regardless of our differences." We aren't trying to erase our differences but rather to accept and respect them, while finding commonalities. We are reading each other as we would listen: to better understand those with whom we share this earth and to see how we can live together more harmoniously.

Without reading each other, without listening, what chance do we have of arriving at our goal?

I don't believe that creating this project is exceptional. In a healthy, democratic society, what we are doing would be commonplace. And that which is the most commonplace may also be the most essential, if not the most sacred. As sacred as the fundamental actions of our existence: breathing, eating, listening. And reading.

But people also write to transform themselves. Somewhere inside of us, we believe that we are our thoughts. We identify with the thoughts in our heads without even knowing where they come from, and when we write, we can perceive, formulate, and deepen these thoughts that shape our lives. We are daily at the mercy of ideas and sentiments that we rarely have the opportunity to question. The demands of life leave little time to know ourselves. But writing can be a personal ritual that allows us to have a deeper understanding of who we are. It can create a space in which our inner lives can become clearer. It can even allow us, in certain ways, to decide who we want to be.

We inherited a language and a culture that we didn't choose and that we can hardly perceive, given how completely immersed within it we are. We often believe that our experience of life is an absolute reality; we believe that our experiences and culture are those which are truest, because they are all that we know. This is why we are writing to interrogate that heritage. Years ago, someone told me, "When you write, try to evoke the country you know best as if it was a foreign and unknown place." All that we take for granted, all that we think is normal, absolute, and true, is but habit. We have to learn to perceive what we take as normal as if we were standing outside ourselves. To know our thoughts, to know the culture that we have received, writing is a powerful tool.

I also believe that we write to find humility. Everyone should talk about their own prejudices and discrimination as you have. I admire you for everything you have managed to say in your letter. We have inherited a racist culture. We have grown up with histories of distrust, disdain, and rage. We have inherited prejudices and wounds. Who among us can say that he doesn't discriminate or have prejudices, or hasn't been affected by racism? Several years ago, I was speaking with a woman in her sixties who had worked for decades in schools in low-income neighbourhoods of New York City. She told me that she had made constant and concerted effort not to be racist, and then said, "Truly not racist. I tried to uproot the deep racism that we don't even see. I work on that every day to better be able to support the people around me." That is what we should all do. I often observe in myself thoughts that I find racist and I realize that I didn't even choose to have them. I learned them and integrated them into my world view before I even learned the word *racism*.

In one of the previous letters, I wrote about why Whites don't want to recognize their racism and the violence that they have inflicted on Indigenous people. I spoke of jurisprudence – that if Indigenous groups succeeded in regaining their territories in court, this could create a judicial precedent for other Indigenous causes. But there is another reason why Whites refuse to speak of racism and it is possibly more significant: they feel a profound sense of guilt.

This guilt is often difficult to explain to people since it has so many nuances. In the same way that we identify with our thoughts, we also identify unconsciously with our heritage and the actions of our ancestors. Admitting the brutality of our society isn't easy. In each country where I've lived, the people point accusingly at another country nearby to say that the people there are worse. I have rarely met people who know how to criticize themselves. In the United States, the guilt that many Whites feel toward African American people is immense. Many of them know that their country has abused and profited from Americans of African descent, but, oddly, instead of issuing formal apologies or trying to heal wounds, Whites blame African American people. How many times have I heard Whites say that African American are lazy and that they have neither the capacity nor the will to participate in the larger society? I have heard people in Quebec say the same thing about Indigenous people. But it's easy to say this sort of thing when the society has been built on the exclusion of minorities, which renders their participation extremely difficult. And blaming others allows us to pardon ourselves – not only of the abuses of the culture and of our ancestors, but also of the perpetuation of the abuses through our own words and actions.

Today, when one person tells another, "What you just said is racist," the reaction is often negative. We feel almost obliged to refuse to admit our racism, since we live in a hypocritical society, in which being racist is generally seen as horrible while the norms of our society constantly encourage us to hold racist views. This forces us into a constant duality: we pretend not to be racist even while acting like racists. We speak of equality and inclusion, but we constantly avoid people who are different. We choose to consume media that perpetuates the racist stereotypes that we say we don't want to accept. So when someone points out our racism, our reflex is to perpetuate the lie that we aren't racist, since the duality of being and not being racist is our societal norm.

One solution may be this: simple words, letters that try to share openly and explore the thoughts that we claim we don't have.

Here is what I hope for: a society in which one person could tell another, "What you just said is racist," and the other could feel free to respond, "I'm sorry. I didn't realize. I am going to think about this and educate myself about it." And if they don't understand why, they can ask the question with humility: "I would like to have a better understanding of why." We will have to show patience and the willingness to listen to arrive at communication of this nature. We will also have to learn to pardon not only the errors others make, but our own, rather than deny them. We will have to be conscious that who we are isn't absolute; our identities aren't written in stone, and we shouldn't have to feel obliged to hide or justify our errors because we fear that they are a permanent part of our identity. We change. If we identify with our errors, we run the risk of repeating them. In order not to do so, we need the wisdom to see that each of us is an amalgam of language, experience, genetics, and cultural heritage. We can begin to change once we cease to believe that doing so isn't possible.

So we are writing to build trust in ourselves and in others. We are writing to learn from each other and to cultivate compassion. Blaming others serves no purpose, and a sense of culpability rarely leads people to change. We have far more need for concrete actions than for guilt.

We change society by changing ourselves. If we want to evolve, we must change our views – open ourselves, accept letting go of ideas that no longer serve us.

We spoke of freedom. I wish that we were free to recognize our racism so that we can better understand it and heal it. Our fear of racism, our fear of guilt and of being wrong limit us. We fail to speak of our weaknesses.

Many times, I have been racist without realizing. I regret this, and I work to recognize it each time deeply rooted prejudices come to the surface and unconsciously influence the way I make decisions.

I dream of a society in which everyone can express themselves as we are doing in these letters, without fear of being threatened or ignored. To arrive at a society like this – you are right to point this out – we have to invest more resources in education. And we have to reconsider our ideas around the sovereignty of the different groups that compose the country. The Haida people, for instance, who have negotiated a sort of shared jurisdiction with the government of British Columbia, have shown that those who live on a territory have a better understanding of how it should be managed than those who live far away and who aren't directly affected by the consequences of logging and mining.[28]

I am writing you these letters not because I have the answers to problems we are discussing, but because I am looking for them and because, in our words, I am starting to see solutions that I can apply in my life.

I am writing to you because I want a better understanding of the culture I have inherited from my society.

I am writing to you because, when I ask you a question and I feel its urgency, I can't deny the importance of the answer.

And I am writing to you to see more clearly – and to continue to build, in my words – the person who I want to be.

I would like to live in a society where racism is seen

---

28   Tony Penikett, "Six Definitions of Aboriginal Self-Government and the Unique Haida Model," paper prepared for the Action Canada Northern Conferences series, Haida Gwaii, September 2012, accessed January 2018, 11 pp., http://www.actioncanada.ca/wp-content/uploads/2014/04/Haida-Gwaii -Governance-EN-Oct-2012.pdf.

as a sickness and where, instead of ineffectively punishing those who are ill, we find lasting ways to heal our society. Thank you for this exchange. I am also writing to say this.

Deni

P.S. Given that you live between two cultures – that of the non-Indigenous Québécois and of the Indigenous community – can you describe the similarities you see between the two groups as well as their differences? How do you think they can understand each other better? The question might seem simple, but I am wondering what I fail to see. What do I not know that I should?

22

My dear Deni, nuitsheuakan,

Build a society, together. I believe we want the same thing, my friend, and I believe that we are both working to inspire that dream in other people around us. I believe that that inspiration is not pointless. On the contrary, it is reaching more and more individuals in our circles, in Quebec and all over the world.

As a matter of fact, we aren't all that different. Our communities aren't so different. Who watches hockey the most, the games of the Canadiens? People make jokes about the fact that hockey is sacred on the reserves. Recently, there was even a controversy in one community about a political leader who allegedly dipped into the funds of the band council to buy tickets to a Canadiens games for his family. I never found out what happened with that. But it made me laugh. On our reserve, some people are ready to drive ten hours to Montreal just to see one Canadiens game. They always stop in Quebec City. We all have some family members in the "Old Capital."

My grandfather Fontaine was a fan of the hockey games on TV. He was known in the village to be one of the biggest Canadiens fans. He never saw them live, as far as I know. Even so, he had a lot of Canadiens memorabilia. I remember my father even told me that, when he was in primary school, grandpa convinced him, him and his brothers, that he had once been a member of the Canadiens team. My father said that he and his brothers really believed him and that they were so proud of it that one of them even did an oral presentation on their father, the former Canadiens player! I had a good laugh the first time I heard that story.

You know, we're a people that loves to laugh. For centuries, the other Indigenous Peoples of America nicknamed us (yes! yes!) "those-who-love-to-laugh." We laugh so much! Our way of laughing is very amusing. And Innu jokes are really hilarious, and the Innu-aimun language takes things even farther, with its clarifications and its nuances, without holding back. I believe that laughter is what saved us. It is written in our genes. You walk around in the communities, in the summer, on our reserves, and you often hear bursts of laughter from a house or a veranda when people are sitting to pass the time of day. Because that's life. Life means taking time. Taking the time to be. Taking the time to laugh. All things that are in conflict with the outside world.

That's not something negative. Quite the contrary. It's our weapon against the darkness. It's what transcends the wound. What generates resilience. We transmit it in our blood, from generation to generation. We don't forget what we are, even though, in certain cases, the government plans to strip us of our humanity have been realized.

What don't you know that you should know?

Now, we're making progress. You and I. And we, my people and I, are also making progress. My country and I, we are also making progress.

I believe that the Québécois and the Indigenous Peoples are a lot alike, as I believe Canadians and Indigenous Peoples living on Canadian territory have a lot in common. At heart, the territory is our first point in common. I believe that we have to find a way to put young people from the two cultures in contact, because they already have similar ideas. They're concerned about the same future, the same society, the same territory. Maybe older people will follow suit. And we'll have at least tried to do something for a better future! A future that is the least racist possible. As open as possible to the world and to the other. If we don't set ourselves clear goals and if we aren't realistic, it'll be difficult to achieve our ideals.

You know, it's a strange kind of life, always sitting between "two chairs," to be constantly dancing between two shores. But I persist in believing that things happen for a reason. I was born Innu, a daughter of ancient traditions, I was born in the city, I no longer speak any languages fluently other than French. Like many other people who have a similar history, I have a feeling that the way is opening up. The way to the other. Our mentalities cross the borders that our languages once erected between them. Now we know how to speak French or English. Now we use different means of expression. We are beginning a profound process of reconciliation with ourselves. We are healing our wounds, our inner racism, and all our anger passed on through blood.

As part of this process, artists in all disciplines will provide help that is both crucial and wonderful. Through this new freedom of expression, the first thing we need to do is free ourselves from the concept of the reserve. Break with the intention that is at the origin of that very concept. A huge endeavour, certainly, but not impossible to achieve if we reverse the logic of it. There is a real eagerness for an overall change in the policies that have disadvantaged us for decades. It will be a matter of emancipating words. Emancipating our identity from the claws of racism, raising it in the cradle of the earth, and giving it life on the physical territory of Quebec. The territory that we share, the territory where we cohabit.

We are so much alike! Young Indigenous people who live in the city are taking more and more interest in Quebec culture, politics, and literature. They have developed a critical eye in comparing the two communities, and not in a negative way. An encounter between two cultures always generates mutual enrichment, a transculturation. We have to break the current imbalance. We have to get the Québécois interested in Indigenous cultures. Help them get to know their nuances and their richness. To have Indigenous heritages acknowledged in Quebec culture. That could be another crucial stage in the process of emancipation of mentalities.

I want to continue my reflection, but I'll let you react first. We still have a few little things to name, I believe.

What do you think? And what about your side? What then is your relationship with the idea of Indigeneity, now that I have revealed so many secrets to you?

How do you perceive us now? Tell me.

Kuessipan!
Hugs,
Natasha

23

Kuei, nuitsheuakan,

The story of your grandfather made me laugh! I can perfectly imagine him telling his sons how he once played for "*les Canadiens*," as well as their pride and the presentation they gave in class. The story is one that reminds us of our shared humanity. And what a classic Québécois story!

For me, to explain my perception of Indigeneity requires that I share more about the experiences that led me to where I am today. Racism is so thoroughly woven into the fabric of our lives that I have spent years trying to understand it.

If I have already talked about my father several times, it's because I have many memories of his racism. He was a philanderer and often spoke of his attraction to Asian women. When I was in the city with him, he pointed out those he found beautiful and told me, "I'd really like to be with an Asian woman, but I wouldn't want to have children with Asian blood." I have a clear memory of the confusion created by his words. I simply didn't understand. I often thought about what he'd said, since I couldn't manage to make sense of it.

When I moved to Virginia, I encountered a much more aggressive racism. Whites, seeing my confusion, tried to tell me the reasons they thought African American people were inferior. At home, my mother said that Whites were ignorant racists, but even today, when I think back to the

African American students in my school in Virginia, I realize how little I knew about them or their lives. About White kids, however, I knew a great deal. There was an immense divide between the lives of the White and African American students, and a deeply ingrained distrust.

Today, I recall their faces and names, as well as many of the interactions I had with them. I remember that, when I became a delinquent, I began hanging out with a group of White boys who were often involved in criminal activity, and one of the African American boys in our school stopped me in the hallway and said, "You're not like those boys, D. [this was what the African American kids called me]. You shouldn't be hanging out with them." I didn't know what he was seeing, but his words made me realize that I didn't understand much about the situation I was in. I had grown up elsewhere, and I failed to grasp the social codes of that region. The African American kids knew how to identify White racists. But I had been living among the racists, hearing and eventually repeating their jokes, as well as those that my racist stepfather liked to tell.

I recall one racist joke in particular that my stepfather told me. I repeated it in school, without realizing that one of my African American classmates was sitting in the corner. One of the White kids gestured, and from it, I could tell that he wasn't bothered by the joke itself, since most of the White kids I knew told them, but he was simply warning me as to our classmate's presence. The African American student said nothing, and it was at that moment that I knew that we could all, like most Whites I knew, embody a hypocritical duality: we repeated racist jokes without thinking about their meaning, without connecting them to the human beings to whom they referred. It was a horrible moment, and it remains painful to think about the harm I caused. It is one of those moments when I began to realize how much I had been influenced by the racist culture in which I lived. I knew Whites who spent hours listening to rap music with African American kids and yet who had no hesitation telling racist jokes about them. It was as if the culture that we had received would express itself through us if we didn't actively try to understand it and negate it. I almost never talk about these memories. They disgust me. Just thinking about them makes me sick. But if I want others to change, to look at themselves and become conscious of the racism throughout our society, I see no choice but to speak frankly about it – and above all about what shames me and makes me uncomfortable.

The racism of my youth was so normalized. Even our teachers made suggestively racist comments or jokes. One day, a few years after I had moved to Virginia, a student brought a White power newspaper to class in my middle school and, when I expressed concern about it, the teacher told me that I couldn't understand since I came from some-where else. The general reaction of my peers was that I simply didn't get it. Today, I think of the many times during those years that adults sat down with me and explained in detail why I should be racist and why I shouldn't have African American friends. Since my mother encouraged me not to be racist, I would repeat her words to them, and they would patiently tell why she was wrong – why racism was normal and why they were justified in hating African American people.

When I hear Whites talk about slavery in the United States, they often speak as if they – had they lived during that time – would have been different from other Whites of the era. But the truth is that the majority of them would have been just as racist as the majority of White people were back then, since that was the culture of the time and, in many ways, still is today. Not following the dominant culture requires immense courage. Not being racist demands that we are conscious of the racism that contaminates nearly all levels of our society.

There's a story that makes me aware of how much racism remains in our culture, even among educated liberals. A friend, the Man Booker Prize–winning novelist Marlon James, once told me that it bothers him when White people say that racism is getting better – that we're much less racist than we used to be. For him, it was completely idiotic to make such an argument: "That's like saying, 'I don't shit in my pants as much as I did when I was a baby.' No, we're adults. We don't shit in our pants anymore. If you're a baby, you can say it's getting better. That's normal. But when you're an adult, you know it's wrong, and you stop it. Why should we pardon a behaviour that we know is wrong and disgusting? We just need to eliminate it altogether." Later, he told me, "Progress implies evolution from one legit state to another, or that it's legit enough that we accept progress as the way out of it. If my kid is sucking his thumb in public, fine I'll wait for him to progress out of it. But if he's pulling out his dick in public, I'm going to say cut that shit out now. Some things you progress out of, some things you need to stop immediately."

The worst was that the words Marlon was critiquing had come out of my own mouth and the mouths of many of my friends in the past – people who were educated and didn't think they were racist. But he was right. By saying that the situation was getting better, White people were accepting persistent racism and were demonstrating their White privilege, since they wouldn't be the ones to suffer from the situation they were discussing. But for African American people, who still endure the worst forms of racism, it would be difficult to affirm so casually that the situation has improved.

All this is to say that if I'd lived two hundred years ago, I almost certainly wouldn't have been free of the racism of that era. If I had been raised with the belief that slavery is normal, I would probably have bought human beings and abused them. It is important to say this so that we remember that we're the products of our culture – one that remains infested with racism. Changing this requires an effort to make ourselves conscious of the situation. It means ending passivity and actively engaging.

Another moment when I understood the extent of the racism that persists in the United States took place as I was walking down the street on a date with an African American woman in New York City and a passing White man called me "a nigger lover." I had been naive not to expect behaviour of this sort in a city as multiethnic as New York. Until then, my Whiteness had exempted me from such aggressive racism, and I understood that, for many minorities, hardly a day passes when they aren't reminded of racism. For Whites, the problem is largely invisible and exists as stories in the media and on Facebook. Whites are generally cut off from that reality and protected from it by the racist institutions of our society.

Another time when I learned a great deal about racism was during my stay in the Democratic Republic of the Congo, where I had gone to research a book. The Congolese have suffered greatly from racism. From 1885 to 1908, Belgium enslaved much of the population, killing people and creating conditions that led to the deaths of millions. After that period, Belgium subjected them to a particularly brutal form of colonialism. The Democratic Republic of the Congo is one of the countries that has the most mineral deposits, and for decades, Belgium, as well as the United States, has tried to control it to better exploit its natural wealth.

The Congolese often told me about the colonial attitudes

that still dominate in their country. They experience it today with international non-governmental organizations (NGOs) that do projects there, whether for nature conservation or other causes that should, in principle, help the local population. They have explained to me that Whites rarely ask for their views and act as if they are better informed to run projects in the Congo, even if they have very little experience there. They described how Whites use their NGO funding to pay for meals or to buy whatever is necessary for their comfort, whereas if the Congolese employees do the same thing, they are immediately accused of corruption. For Whites, what they consider corruption among others is so normal in their own practices that they often don't even see it as such. The Congolese also spoke of Whites who sent them on expeditions in the rainforest with ridiculously small budgets because they figured that the Congolese could survive in nature without boots, tents, or other materials of which the Whites would never have deprived themselves. The Whites treated them as if they were half-animal, as if they didn't have the same human needs, whereas it should go without saying that the Congolese found the expeditions to be extremely demanding and tiring – especially if they had to do them without adequate resources.

One story in particular made a strong impression on me.[29] The small NGO about which I was writing – whose success was built on its relationships with the Congolese and its respect for their culture – had received a grant to dig a village well in the nature reserve where they were working. There are many NGOs in Africa that specialize in digging wells, some of which claim that they dig hundreds

---

29   I wrote about this in my book, published as *Of Bonobos and Men: A Journey to the Heart of the Congo* in the United States (Minneapolis: Milkweed Editions, 2013) and *The Last Bonobo: A Journey Into the Congo* in Canada (Windsor, Ontario: Biblioasis, 2015).

every year – and, of course, thousands of African villages need wells to provide clean water. But in villages without wells, the women are generally those who are responsible for going to the river each day to get water – a chore that strikes many Westerners as particularly onerous. In this case, when the small NGO asked the villagers if they wanted a well, the men immediately agreed, whereas the women looked more hesitant as they said yes. The NGO directors had been expecting the women to be happy to be freed from having to get water each day. And yet there was no sign of contentment on their faces as they accepted the well project. Later, one of the NGO workers spoke with the women when they were away from the men and asked them how the well would change their lives. The women responded that if there was a well, they would no longer be able to leave the village to go to the river and would be stuck with the men all day. For them, the best part of their day was going to the river, where they met sisters, cousins, and aunts who lived in nearby villages. While bathing and washing clothes, they sang and gossiped about the men. During that time, their children played together. Listening to that story, I could imagine generations of children who played at the river and went on to become leaders in their communities. If one day there was a conflict between villages over resources, the leaders would more easily be able to resolve it, having known each other since childhood. If we begin to cut the bonds between villages, what would become of the culture of the people?

I am writing about this because it's also a question of racism. Whites often believe that they know better than others. They project their culture and way of seeing the world onto foreign countries, and their actions often destroy the pre-existing cultural equilibrium. I have heard dozens of stories of this sort. For instance, in Afghanistan,

I learned that Afghan soldiers who attacked the American soldiers with whom they worked didn't, in general, do so because they were under the influence of the Taliban, but rather because they constantly felt insulted by the American soldiers who blew their noses and passed gas in public, as well as patted Afghans on the back to say, "Good job!" In Afghan culture, these three actions are considered serious insults. Even worse was that American soldiers sometimes pointed their weapons toward Afghans without realizing they were doing so, whereas, in Afghan culture, pointing a weapon at someone is a way of saying, "I am going to kill you." The United States military spent more than ten years in Afghanistan before becoming aware of such problems and trying to resolve them. Their cultural arrogance had blinded them, and, in many ways, they acted as if they already knew everything necessary to do their job. This sense of superiority is deeply rooted in Western culture.

This sort of racism – of superiority – remains as present in Europe as in North America. It brings to mind a time when I was at the Brussels Book Fair, where I had been invited to participate in a discussion about the African Great Lakes in Central Africa. However, there wasn't a single African writer on the panel. I was shocked (though, after all that you and I have discussed, I shouldn't have been) that, in 2015, a group of Whites would come together to discuss potential solutions for problems in Africa, without inviting any African thinkers to participate. I couldn't see the point of our discussion. Moreover, many African writers could have participated, especially in Belgium where the Congolese community remains strong.

When I speak, when I act, I try to connect my words and ideas to the people to whom they refer. I try to see if what I am expressing is accurate. And often, I have to admit that it isn't. My words and those of many White people I

125

know are often the continuation of racism that has long existed in our society – the continuation of racial violence and oppression that emerges from that language. In the wake of every racist joke, every racist gesture, every racist project, there are murders. This isn't an exaggeration, as you know. Many people are excluded from a society in which they would have liked to participate. There are voices that we will never hear. And we, in the West, who believe ourselves to be the protectors of democracy, we should know that if we don't listen to the voices of the diverse groups who constitute our society, then we aren't living in a true democracy. How can we make decisions for our collective future if we can't listen respectfully to numerous diverging points of view? Democracy isn't the simple act of voting. It also implies informing oneself about the complex social issues of the time and hearing the diverse perspectives of those who are involved, and then choosing the best path forward. Voting in ignorance serves no purpose.

So to respond to your question – after many detours – my idea of Indigeneity is connected to openness. I want to learn. I am open, as I am to the many ethnic groups on this earth, though more so, since I share this country with Indigenous people and, in better understanding your culture, I can understand more clearly how we can live together. I perceive Indigenous people as a diverse group, with rich cultures. You are a person different from all others, and there are millions of ways of being Indigenous just as there are millions of ways of being White. I am always trying to continue learning, to better discern the humanity of others so that I can dismantle the cultural prejudices that obscure people from each other. I try not to reduce people to an idea or erase individuality with my words, though I know that I have. What would my writing be worth if it amounted to that? With each book, I try to continue growing. For me, writing is the act of opening.

In a few years, I will surely reread this book and realize how ignorant I was when I wrote it. Maybe I will receive letters from our readers who will tell me that my way of seeing the world could be more open. I hope so.

Natasha, we are coming to the end of our project, and yet many subjects remain that we haven't discussed. Several times, in your letters, you mentioned genocide. This is a difficult subject to address for White people, since many of us associate it with Germany, the Second World War, and the Nazi extermination of the Jews. There are few White people in North America who are ready to admit that a genocide happened here. One of the primary divides between our people is our distinct histories. The majority of Whites have no interest in the history of Indigenous Peoples, since, in it, the image of the White person is generally negative. But how can we live together well without knowing and respecting each other's histories? This would be painful for many Whites, but raising the barrier of history would help us in the long term.

What are your thoughts on this?

Kuessipan!
Deni

24

Kuei, kuei, Deni,

I often wonder how long it will take us to open our eyes and to free ourselves from all these psychological straitjackets. We tell each other stories, we exchange information. And yet, you've helped me discover other perspectives that show that racism exists not only in America, but everywhere in the world. And everywhere it is sustained by the loathsome mechanisms of neocolonialism.

Now we are spectators of a global crisis that affects the entire planet: economic crisis, environmental crisis, social crisis, spiritual crisis … We can expect global warming to produce disasters until there is a generalized humanitarian crisis. With all the terrorist alerts currently looming over Western countries, with those countries themselves very involved in the wars in the Middle East, it seems that hope is becoming as rare as mountain water.

These events have brought me to understand that processes of colonization, wherever they take place, feed much of the current resentments and revolts. I've been rather sad since I became aware of this tangle of causes. Your letters have permitted me to expand my world view, beyond Quebec and Canada.

I'm reflecting on everything, asking myself questions about everything. Sometimes, I wonder if my relationship with decolonization is correct. I try to be colonized as little as possible, but I'm afraid of getting it wrong. As if I had to doubt this intuition before taking action and decolonizing myself for good. Of course, I detached myself a long time ago from the system of material consumption, which runs on "compulsiveness." I no longer buy anything in the big stores. I reuse what I find. It's a way to respect my ecological consciousness and to escape the social pressure to consume more and more.

Since I've been learning our history, listening to the narrative of our past events, internalizing our various myths and legends, retracing our memories, I've been reconstituting my personal fable. I've reconstituted the material elements, but also the imaginary, cultural, and spiritual aspects. I am restructuring the movement of the migrations of our peoples on a mental map. I am recreating the country as it appeared in the time of grandiose landscapes and majestic trees. The country with its deep, ancient roots. The real continent, in our full consciousness of it.

And what if we dared think about that dreamed-of country the way we think, yes, about all the existing political and government institutions in which power is so frightening? If, in our minds, we caused the land and the territory, its body and its epidermis to rumble? What if we made them dance before the howls of fear and the gnashing of teeth that that dreamed-of country seems to provoke?

Which brings me back to the question of genocide. As I mentioned before, we now know that the roots of colonization are still very much alive. But there always comes a time when a system built on unhealthy foundations is no longer able to perpetuate itself. One day, we will finally see a resurgence of the great survival instinct of humanity. I hope so, anyway.

In my lectures, I often talk about this idea of the "survival instinct." For me, the great leadership of the women in the cross-Canada Indigenous movement Idle No More can be explained precisely by the instinct and intuitions of those Indigenous women, who have generally stayed much closer to our traditional lifestyle (even though that lifestyle is no longer the same). The genetics are so strong that the simple fact of being the descendant of an ancient nomadic tradition, of a way of thinking based on what is essential, reinforces the feeling that transmission is what will save us.

A great genocide has been taking place in North America for five centuries. If you want to have an insider's view, I suggest you read *Touch the Earth*,[30] an anthology of statements and accounts of Indigenous leaders from the 1700s and 1800s. The first time I opened that book, I was with my best friend. We were in the stacks of a library in Rimouski, and as soon as we read a page, we sank to the floor and started weeping. In silence. It really hit us hard. Maybe we carried memories in our DNA. The memory of the Great Wound. Of the Great Split.

The "earth" referred to in the title of the book is all the sacred land in the Americas. From the northern most reaches of North America's Ellesmere Island (Umingmak Nuna) in Canada's Nunavut to the southern tip of South America's Tierra del Fuego. The physical territory and spirit of Americas. I'm not going to repeat the cliché of our ancestral vision of the beings that make up our environment. But I'm convinced: it's this earth that we drink, its animals are what we eat. It is its roots that have fed us and healed us for ten thousand years. We developed a great, rich relationship with it. An extraordinary relationship that every human being should know and accept. A relationship we should commit ourselves to. In order to survive.

---

30   T.C. McLuhan, *Touch the Earth: A Self-portrait of Indian Existence* (New York: Promontory Press, 1992).

When the Europeans "landed" on the sacred earth, nightmares and oracles of spiritual guides (shamans) had already been haunting us for ages. We'd been warned. The ceremonies were full of warnings and worries. We tried to stop the Europeans, escape their massacres. I imagine that we also tried to transmit certain teachings to them so they would know how to survive on the land they intended to settle on. We tried to do it, to live together with them.

And they came and built their villages. They arrived by boatloads, more and more numerous. More and more sure of themselves. We saw them starting to build things everywhere. We saw them mould the earth. To exploit it or just to survive. They erected walls around their villages. Of course they were afraid! We were scared too.

I'll stop here. If I continue describing to you all the visions I get, my heart will burst. I will reopen my wound, which has healed poorly. You know, it's the first time I've tried to imagine the first impressions that my people must have felt: the fear, the questioning, the survival instinct … To describe that intuition that lets you foresee that what comes next will be very harmful for environmental harmony. That harmony that our peoples had preserved from generation to generation and of which they are still today the defenders.

To talk about the genocide that my people have known can be long and painful. In short, let's say that what was to follow were land grabs, trade across the continent, negotiations, thefts, massacres. Revolts. More massacres. Blankets infected with epidemic diseases. Death. They decimated us everywhere in the Americas. Then there was the movement west, the gold rush, and so forth. The search for oil sources. The extraction of natural resources, clearcutting. The exploitation of the lands. In my memory, all of history is speeding up. What would the country have become had there never been a conquest? Genocide is the expression of a will to kill humans. To eradicate them. To wipe them out. To erase their presence in the world. And what if we set out now on the conquest of authenticity? Of true history, first of all, then of our humanity?

Since I've been writing to you about my inner racism, I don't know how to take the necessary distance to get rid of it. But I'll take the time to do it. I will feed my poetry and the last messages of revolt that I still have to deliver to your people about this metamorphosis. With time, everything changes, everything goes away. We have to take the time. It's unbelievable. I never would have imagined that. But with you, everything is revealed. With our conversations, the light that we are kindling is warming me.

Then I'll undertake the search for the path that will lead me to my own reconciliation. Repair myself first, repair my wounds, my personal Wound of Colonization. Then look for myself, set out on a quest for my face and finally reach the starting point of my personal reconciliation.

When I've found myself – I swear to you that I want to do it as quickly as possible, but while respecting my own pace, without getting overwhelmed – I'll get down to work on reconciliation with you and between our peoples.

We are coming to the end of the first stage of our new relationship: dialogue.

Kuessipan, my friend,
Natasha

25

Kuei Natasha,

You are right to point out that colonial attitudes pervade everything that we do. The first step is to be conscious of this. Today, countries of the Western world often accuse – with good reason – other countries of genocide, but we refuse to admit that a genocide also took place here, in the Americas. Our governments don't want to make reparations, and yet the definition that the United Nations gives for genocide is: "... acts committed with intent to destroy, in whole or in part, a national, ethnic, racial or religious group ..."[31] In light of that definition, and after having read even a little of Canada's history, it seems that we can easily conclude that a genocide took place here – as well as a cultural genocide for the Indigenous people who survived, as the Truth and Reconciliation Commission of Canada itself affirmed in its report. Even if we can't right past wrongs, we can nonetheless recognize the history of Indigenous people and respect their suffering, and take action to change the current situation.

Even as we feel the urgent need for this change, we

---

31   United Nations General Assembly, Resolution 260 A (III), Convention on the Prevention and Punishment of the Crime of Genocide, Article 2 (December 9, 1948), p. 1, http://www.un.org/en/genocideprevention/documents /atrocity-crimes/Doc.1_Convention%20on%20the%20Prevention%20and%20 Punishment%20of%20the%20Crime%20of%20Genocide.pdf.

have to be perseverant in our actions to create it. When I was younger, I would often get an idea and would want to achieve it instantly. As a result, I would tire or burn myself out, since I felt that my efforts could never match the goal I had set for myself. When we dream of revolutions and great transformations, it's easy to have the impression that nothing is changing, since our society is so far from that of which we dream. I have seen this infuriate and discourage many people. They are so determined to see change that they exhaust many of the people around them and attack those who could have been their allies. And there are also those who want to see change without making much effort or getting their hands dirty.

Over the last ten years, I have travelled to more than sixty countries, since I was eager to learn and meet people from around the world. Even if I have spoken of colonial attitudes throughout the world, I have also met extraordinary people. In the book I wrote about the Democratic Republic of the Congo, I explain how I came to understand – to truly, deeply understand – that "poverty does not equate to ignorance." I met many White people – Americans, Canadians, Québécois, and Europeans – who had integrated this way of thinking. They invested much of their time listening to others, learning as much as possible.

I have also seen that the activists who help create the most change are often those who have realized that they have to live in this world to change it. This doesn't mean accepting the system. We should never accept or pardon a system that causes or perpetuates injustice. Nor should we hesitate to give up comfort or privileges to stop oppression. But as inspired as we can be by this feeling of urgency, we must first understand society before being able to change it – above all if we don't want to reproduce its failures.

Changes are often the result of many small actions. There

is the expression, "God is in the details." I'm not religious, but this expression speaks to me: even if we have a clear and powerful vision that we aspire to create, it is still necessary, day after day, to work on the many small changes that will allow us to arrive at it. The greatest activists are often those who are most attentive to details and who know how to cultivate human relations even as they work on themselves.

When I look at my own path, I sometimes feel as if I've succeeded in changing. At other times, I have the impression that nothing has changed despite my efforts. Then, all of a sudden, I realize to what degree I am no longer the same person. Writing this book is one step toward transformation. The people that we will become will be the results of the choices that we take today. And we have the freedom and awareness to choose how we wish to nourish our minds.

Through these letters – by sharing and learning – I believe that we are creating something bigger than ourselves. The majority of Whites have, in general, few occasions in their lives when they will meet Indigenous people, and it is also with them that we are establishing this dialogue. Writing can be action; it can even be activism. Social movement and revolutions often start with manifestos and various writings, since it is important to identify and name the actions necessary to change individual minds and society as a whole. We first have to trace the path. The barriers between Whites and Indigenous people may seem immense, but small gestures can dismantle them – even letters between friends.

Our letters have also given me the opportunity to think through the sorts of actions that can be taken to combat racism. As a non-Indigenous person and writer, I realize that it's important for me to listen to voices that haven't been sufficiently heard and to draw attention to them.

While we were writing these letters, I kept a notebook

of ideas and responses, and I would like to share some of what remains in it.

– A growing number of Canadians understand the situation in Palestine. Before, the majority of Canadians that I knew spoke of Palestinians as terrorists and blamed them for the conflict with Israel. But I hear more Canadians (as well as Americans, Jewish people, and even Israelis) expressing their awareness that the Palestinians' territories have been confiscated and their human rights violated. In certain ways, I think that we can address a parallel with Indigenous Peoples of North America. In recent years, Canada, like Israel, has ignored critiques by international organizations like the United Nations and Amnesty International that address its treatment of Indigenous people. While Canadians take time to admit the reality of the crimes, each day that passes is an act of violence against Indigenous people – a denial of their existence. Ignoring the problem will not cause it to vanish.

– I was thinking about what you wrote with regard to technology in one of your letters. You were right to say that it reduces empathy. There are now studies that show this. However, new technology is becoming integrated with our lives, whether we want it or not, and it has the power to open windows on realities very different from our own. It can create virtual communities that bring together not only Indigenous people on one side or Whites on the other, but both in a united discussion if that is what we choose. We have to recognize that, if Facebook didn't exist, I would have known much less about you and your projects early in our friendship. To my eyes, you would have remained a person I met in the literary world and I wouldn't have been as aware of your activism. Here, as elsewhere, technology is facilitating social movements.

– We also have to think about our own history and the social origins of our behaviour. At the time of colonization, there was a belief in Europe that White people were the chosen race. When the colonists arrived in America and saw the Indigenous people dying of the diseases they'd brought from Europe, many of them believed that God was eliminating those who weren't chosen. The Anglo-Saxons even believed that they were the only chosen people and that all others were inferior races destined for extinction. They conceived of the "New World" as a new biblical revelation, a new promised land. Writings of that era suggest that non-European people will naturally die off to create space. This in part explains why European colonists kept them at a distance in many ways. Today, many North American towns and cities continue to distance Indigenous communities from their centres and the services that could benefit them. In light of this, it is dangerous to ignore our histories when we are trying to understand our actions today, as many old cultural beliefs create situations that continue to influence us and that reinforced the racist social structures that have grown into those we have today.

– To continue with the idea from the preceding note: White people often forget how truly closed their society remains to Indigenous people and how many negative perceptions still exist. I would like that White readers of this book take a moment to imagine entering somewhere – it could be a school or a workplace – where people are constantly distrustful of them, or are afraid of them without any clear reason, or simply express open dislike toward them. In the process of writing these letters, I have considered how truly difficult this must be to experience. And yet it is what millions of Indigenous people, African American, and immigrants experience daily. I can imagine how this could make bettering their lives or living among White people a challenge.

– Whites have to recognize passive and silent racism: the indifference and the lack of interest for those who live near them as well as the degree to which people remain closed to their problems and their points of view. The fact that racism is silent doesn't mean that it isn't active, that it doesn't have an impact on the world. Even many of the White people who speak out against racism on Facebook often live in relatively closed communities. We have to find ways to take action. As Marlon James, the Jamaican novelist I quoted earlier in the book, explained in a video for the *Guardian*'s website: "It's not enough to be non-racist. We have to be antiracist." He goes on to say, "We need to accept that what hurts one of us hurts all of us."[32] Both Whites and people of colour are harmed by racism, even though in different ways. The racism of the Québécois toward Indigenous people also harms the Québécois: through anger, through regret, through guilt, and through isolation. But the

---

32   Marlon James, "Are you racist? 'No' isn't a good enough answer – video," *The Guardian*, January 13, 2016, video, 2:05, https://www.theguardian.com /commentisfree/video/2016/jan/13/marlon-james-are-you-racist-video.

more we make space for others, the more we will create space for ourselves. The more that Quebec will be open to Indigenous people, the more Quebec will be open to Whites as well. We often fail to realize how much the oppression of others also harms us.

– I ask myself how people can undo their racism if, after having considered other points of view, they still feel anger or disdain for them. During a difficult period in my life, when I was questioning my beliefs and values, I began doing an exercise in which I would begin trying to visualize the logical conclusions of thoughts or actions. I would attempt to imagine all of the consequences that might follow, and I was at times surprised by how much resulted, how long the effects were for each cause. Often, I noticed that a thought or an attitude that gave me satisfaction in the short term made me unhappy in the long term or was harmful to others. Even if the behaviour in question gave me a feeling of being in control or of having power, I could see clearly – by following the series of consequences in my head – that the harm I created around me would return to me. Even if I couldn't succeed in feeling empathy or compassion, I was able to rationally recognize that my behaviour, ultimately, did nothing good for society. It made me realize that the first step in taking action is to cease nourishing thoughts whose conclusions are harmful for others and for myself. Over time, doing this mental exercise helped me feel more empathy for others, and I could sense, as well as see, how much my actions would affect them.

I still question myself about the reasons that push me to write. People have often asked me the question. In truth, I write above all to learn and to transform myself. When I write, I see my unconscious self expressed in words and I can better understand who I am. In my life, my primary passion has been learning so that I cannot be trapped within my own thoughts and perceptions. Year after year, I have a better understanding of what I don't know. I am more skilled at asking questions and listening to the answers. I recognize that it is in difference that we find solutions we couldn't have otherwise imagined. I realize that the world that I know is the one I have built, with the knowledge I hold. We can choose to live in a world that is constricted and suffocating, or in one that is open and expansive. But to do that, we first need the humility to recognize the degree to which we are limited by our thoughts. By engaging in dialogue, we learn to know ourselves, as in the philosophy of Socrates, and, by having a better understanding of our strengths and weaknesses, perhaps we can gradually become masters of ourselves. "Nitipenimitishun." We can become free.

I also question my dreams. What are they? I certainly dream of a world in which people realize at last that to take action is not so difficult, and in which they don't expect others to do things in their place. Each conversation and discussion that we have, each project that we accomplish can provoke change. I dream of living among people who desire to learn and who aren't afraid of realizing that they aren't always right. I dream of living in a society where our errors don't oblige us to take paths that lead us away from each other. It's enough to admit them to continue our lives together. In my ideal society, I can see myself being wrong and people having enough compassion to tell me. I see no other way for us to liberate ourselves from the constraints and the limits that our culture and our ancestors have passed on to us.

Natasha, I believe that you will become an important figure in your activism for both Indigenous and White communities – which is to say, all of Quebec, as well as in Canada and the world. Since I have known you, I can see how clearly you are learning and expanding your perspective on life and on yourself. The best leaders are those who understand the points of view of multiple communities and societies, and you are well placed to do this.

I look forward to following your work in the years to come.

Iame uenapissish, nuitsheuakan.
Deni

26

Deni,

We've come to the end of this exchange. However, there are still so many things that we could say and discuss. But if the dialogue that we've begun can help to inspire the reflections of our contemporaries, then we'll really have come to the end of our correspondence. We'll have achieved our objective. Meanwhile, all we can do is continue to follow current events, discussions, and reactions on the subject. In fact, it seems that lately news about Indigenous issues has been more and more present in the public arena. We'll see in time what our exchange will contribute to that discussion.

Since our last meeting at the North Shore Book Fair in April 2015, things have been happening very, very quickly. I'm thinking of the Truth and Reconciliation Commission, which, in June 2015, finally tabled its voluminous report on the assaults suffered by the children of our peoples during the time of the Canadian Indian residential school system. In total, ninety-four recommendations were submitted to the Canadian government. Like new commandments. I'm also thinking of the courageous public revelations of those Indigenous women who were discriminated against and sexually assaulted by members of the Val-d'Or police. Of the federal election in October 2015, and the ten Indigenous Members of Parliament who were elected to the House of Commons, more than ever before in the history of Canada.

Of the verdict of the Supreme Court that finally recognized the ancestral title for land in British Columbia that a Haida First Nation has been demanding for years. Finally, I'm thinking of the National Inquiry into Missing and Murdered Indigenous Women and Girls launched in December 2015 by the new Liberal government of Justin Trudeau. A year filled with historical events, a year for being Indigenous!

I try to reflect on all the "reparation" work in the history of the First Nations of Canada. I tell myself more and more – and I state it now almost every time I find myself in a public forum – that there cannot be reconciliation without reparation. Because that is where the danger lies: to talk about reconciliation and believing that we have already achieved it, as if all that remained to do was to figure out which horn we should grab our buffalo by. We have to first go through reparation. But how? I think there is another essential stage before that: knowledge. Knowledge of the self, knowledge of the other will be the key to repairing and alleviating the generational pain of our peoples. Acknowledgment too. First of all, acknowledgment that people existed before the arrival of Christopher Columbus in America. And then, understanding that those people, who have been marginalized in Canadian society, are in fact the descendants of the people who were present at the time of the "discovery of the New World."

Acknowledgment. The next stage will be to acknowledge the earth that was dear to our ancestors. I do not believe that human beings will be worthy of that heritage without becoming conscious of the spiritual, philosophical, and human value of the territory.

At the risk of once again appearing too spiritual (anyway, it's part of my cultural and philosophical heritage to be spiritual!), I feel that everyone should now find the humility to ask for healing. The deep healing of our morals, our mentalities, our attitudes. We have to find the capacity to acknowledge our mutual ignorance. We have to seek out a way that will give us the will to follow the path of decolonization. Because all this will not occur without pain. I've asked myself a lot of questions and I've had a lot of doubts in the course of our exchanges, but I think that's a good thing. This means that the work has really begun. That things are moving, both inside us and in the world.

I'm in Paris now and this is my last letter. I travelled to the 2015 United Nations Climate Change Conference in Paris and I've taken part in a major expression of Indigenous perspectives. Here, Indigenous Peoples from around the world are coming together and beginning to exchange, to interact. In the midst of this chaos, I feel at home. This afternoon, the Guarani of South America held a summit on the alliance among peoples for the protection of the territory against *ecocide* – the destruction of Earth's ecosystems.[33] This is the point we've reached today: creating strong, solid links to build planetary communication. We're at the beginning of a great movement of liberation, even though in many respects it seems difficult to achieve. But that's where we are now. That's why it is urgent and important for the populations of Quebec and Canada to open up to the First Peoples of the Americas.

But we shouldn't be satisfied with dialogue between ourselves and reconciling with ourselves. We also have to turn our gaze to the outside and commit ourselves to setting an example in the world. We will have to better define and better affirm our place in the world, like certain Indigenous

---

33   For more information on the theme of "ecocide," see for example Valérie Cabanes's *Un nouveau droit pour la Terre. Pour en finir avec l'écocide*, Collection Anthropocène (Paris: Éditions du Seuil, 2016), as well as Kevin Bales's *Blood and Earth: Modern Slavery, Ecocide, and the Secret to Saving the World* (New York: Spiegel & Grau, 2016).

environmental groups that are now able to universalize their presence and enrich themselves with the resources of contemporary societies.

I'm very happy to have been able to further my understanding with you of many subjects related to racism between Indigenous and non-Indigenous people. It has given me access to the vision of a person who cares about his people as much as I care about mine. Now we can commit ourselves to finding the right answers and the right actions that we should take in the future.

I'll always feel grateful to you. You brought out in me feelings that I had to contend with in my daily life, but I never dared to face them, because I was not necessarily conscious of them. Through our exchanges, I was able to identify my certainties and, above all, my doubts. I'm making progress every day with this new knowledge; of myself and of the other. And of you.

Finally, I believe that I have found in you the same desire to write for posterity. We are writing to map the future for the coming generation. That's reassuring. We also write to further our own thinking, to call into question our own perceptions of the world.

I am anxious to work with you again, if the future allows it. And in a few years, we'll see what will have become of this book. We'll see.

I feel enormous gratitude to you, my friend.

May your path be the right one and everything you have given me in the past year come back to you a hundredfold.

Hugs.
Until the next time,
Natasha

APPENDIX 1

Chronology of Events

APRIL 1, 2014 – A report from the Royal Canadian Mounted Police (RCMP) estimates that one thousand Indigenous women have gone missing or been killed since the 1960s.[34]

FEBRUARY 3, 2015 – A report from the Wellesley Institute, titled *First Peoples, Second Class Treatment* shows that racism is a major factor in the generally poorer health of Indigenous people in Canada.[35]

FEBRUARY 14, 2015 – For the February 14th Women's Memorial March, hundreds of people march in the cities of western Canada in memory of missing and murdered Indigenous women and girls.

JUNE 3, 2015 – After six years of work, during which more than six thousand people testified, the Truth and Reconciliation Commission of Canada submits its report.[36] It concludes that the Canadian Indian residential school system was a key tool in a cultural genocide targeting the First Peoples of Canada. It should be noted that the federal Minister of Aboriginal Affairs and

---

34   Royal Canadian Mounted Police, *Missing and Murdered Aboriginal Women: A National Operational Overview* (Ottawa: Government of Canada, 2014), 23 pp., http://www.rcmp-grc.gc.ca/wam/media/460/original/ocbd8968a049aa0b 44d343e76b4a9478.pdf.

35   Billie Allan and Janet Smylie, *First Peoples, Second Class Treatment: The Role of Racism in the Health and Well-being of Indigenous Peoples in Canada* (Toronto: Wellesley Institute, 2015), 64 pp., http://www.wellesleyinstitute.com /wp-content/uploads/2015/02/Full-Report-FPSCT-Updated.pdf.

36   See Truth and Reconciliation Commission of Canada, *Honouring the Truth, Reconciling for the Future: Summary of the Final Report of the Truth and Reconciliation Commission of Canada* (Ottawa: Government of Canada, December 2015), 536 pp., http://www.trc.ca/websites/trcinstitution/File/2015 /Honouring_the_Truth_Reconciling_for_the_Future_July_23_2015.pdf.

Northern Development, Conservative Bernard Valcourt, remained sitting when the conclusions of the report were announced, unlike all the other people present in the hall.

JUNE 4, 2015 – The Premier of Quebec, Philippe Couillard, recognizes the cultural genocide of the Indigenous Peoples.

JULY 23, 2015 – A report from the United Nations Human Rights Committee denounces violence against the Aboriginal women of Canada.[37]

AUGUST 3, 2015 – The Superior Court of Quebec declares that certain provisions of the Indian Act are discriminatory on the basis of sex, therefore violating Section 15 of the Canadian Charter of Rights and Freedoms.

AUGUST 4, 2015 – A group marches three thousand kilometres in the Canadian West in memory of missing and murdered Indigenous women and girls.

OCTOBER 4, 2015 – The 10th Annual Memorial March and Vigil for Missing and Murdered Native Women and Girls is held in Montreal.

OCTOBER 15, 2015 – The Assembly of First Nations Quebec-Labrador calls for a public inquiry on the violent and unexplained deaths of young Indigenous people that have occurred since 2000.

OCTOBER 22, 2015 – The program *Enquête*, broadcast on the

---

37   See, for example, the online article "UN Human Rights Committee Slams Canada's Record on Women," CBC News, July 23, 2015, accessed January 2018, http://www.cbc.ca/news/canada/un-human-rights-committee -slams-canada-s-record-on-women-1.3164650; and the statement by the Feminist Alliance for International Action, "Joint Statement: Canada Must Take Action on the United Nations Rights Committee's Concluding Observations Released Today," July 23, 2015, accessed January 2018, http://fafia-afai.org/en /joint-statement-canada-must-take-action-on-the-united-nations-human -rights-committees-concluding-observations-released-today/.

Radio-Canada network, reveals that Indigenous women and girls have been victims of sexual assaults and intimidation by certain police officers of the Sûreté du Quebec, Quebec's provincial police, in Val-d'Or.[38] The report creates a sensation.

OCTOBER 24, 2015 – A march in solidarity with Indigenous women and girls is held in Val-d'Or.

OCTOBER 29, 2015 – In Montreal, more than 2,000 people take part in a vigil in support of Indigenous women and girls.

NOVEMBER 3, 2015 – The city of Val-d'Or calls for a national inquiry on missing and murdered Indigenous women and girls.

NOVEMBER 4, 2015 – The Quebec government announces investments of six million dollars to improve the living conditions of Indigenous women and girls.

NOVEMBER 10, 2015 – Several First Nations launch a class action suit on behalf of day students of the Canadian Indian residential school system. Unlike former Indigenous live-in students, they have never received an official apology and financial compensation from Canada.

NOVEMBER 17, 2015 – The Committee on Citizen Relations begins consultations in Sept-Îles, Quebec, on the problems of violence experienced by Indigenous women and girls.

NOVEMBER 21, 2015 – Ghislain Picard, leader of the Assembly of First Nations Quebec-Labrador, declares himself a sovereignist at the National Council of the Parti Québécois, which brings him a standing ovation from the gathering. At the press briefing that follows, he specifies that this sovereignty is that of the Innu people.

---

38   *Enquête*, episode aired on October 22, 2015, on Radio-Canada, directed by Emmanuel Marchand, http://ici.radio-canada.ca/tele/enquete/2015-2016/episodes/360817/femmes-autochtones-surete-du-quebec-sq.

NOVEMBER 28, 2015 – The leaders of the Innu nation publish a letter titled "Nous sommes Innus. Nous sommes souverainistes." ("We are Innuat. We are sovereignists.") in support of Ghislain Picard's declaration the week before.

DECEMBER 8, 2015 – The federal government of Justin Trudeau, elected in October, confirms that it will hold a national inquiry on missing and murdered Indigenous women and girls.

DECEMBER 14, 2015 – The association Quebec Native Women publishes a gloomy report on the living conditions of Indigenous women and girls, titled *Nāniawig Māmawe Nīnawind. Stand with Us: Missing and Murdered Indigenous Women in Quebec.*[39]

DECEMBER 15, 2015 – The Truth and Reconciliation Commission publishes its final report on the Canadian Indian residential school system.[40] Close to 3,200 deaths were recorded from 1867 to 2000.

JANUARY 5, 2016 – Ottawa launches an online survey to inform the design of the inquiry on missing and murdered Indigenous women and girls.

JANUARY 14, 2016 – The Canadian Broadcasting Corporation reports that 25.4% of prisoners in federal prisons are Indigenous.[41]

---

39   Femmes autochtones du Québec Inc. / Quebec Native Women Inc., with Annie Bergeron, Alana Boileau, and Carole Lévesque (Kahnawake: Femmes autochtones du Québec Inc. / Quebec Native Women Inc., 2015), 79 pp., http://www.faq-qnw.org/wp-content/uploads/2016/11/Naniawig-Mamawe -Ninawind-Stand-with-us-Oct-2016-engl-FINAL.pdf.

40   Truth and Reconciliation Commission of Canada, *Honouring the Truth, Reconciling for the Future: Summary of the Final Report of the Truth and Reconciliation Commission of Canada* (Ottawa: Government of Canada, December 2015), 536 pp., http://www.trc.ca/websites/trcinstitution/File/2015/Honouring_the _Truth_Reconciling_for_the_Future_July_23_2015.pdf.

41   CBC News, "Prison Watchdog Says More than a Quarter of Federal Inmates Are Aboriginal People," January 14, 2016, http://www.cbc.ca/news /indigenous/aboriginal-inmates-1.3403647.

JANUARY 17, 2016 – In Montreal, a poetry vigil called Paroles fauves ("Wild words") denounces violence against Indigenous women and girls.

JANUARY 28, 2016 – The Saskatchewan Senator Lillian Eva Dyck introduces Bill S-215, "An Act to amend the Criminal Code (sentencing for violent offences against Aboriginal women)" to protect Indigenous women and girls, who are at greater risk of violence.[42]

JANUARY 26, 2016 – The Canadian Human Rights Tribunal accuses the Government of Canada of discriminating against Indigenous children by not giving them the same level of social services as it gives to non-Indigenous children.

---

42   Senate of Canada, *Bill S-215*, first reading (Ottawa: Government of Canada, December 11, 2015), 6 pp., http://www.parl.ca/DocumentViewer /en/42-1/bill/S-215/first-reading.

APPENDIX 2

A Few Words in Innu-aimun

Ancestor | Tshiashinnu

Before | Nikan

Be wounded (s/he has a wound) | Mishkassiu

Compassion | Tshitimatshenimueun

Culture | Aitun

Different | Aitan

Fear | Shetshishun

Fire | Ishkuteu

From one generation to the next | Aianishkat

Future | Aishkat

Girl | Innushkueuss

Goodbye | Niaut *or* iame

Hello | Kuei

History | Tipatshimun

Human being | Innu

Human beings (the Innu People) | Innuat

I love you | Tshishatshitin

In the country, inland | Nutshimit

In the past | Utat *or* ueshkat

Language, speech | Aimun

Laugh (s/he laughs) | Papu *or* ushinam[u]

Legend, myth | Atanukan

Look (s/he looks at it) | Tshitapatam[u]

Me | Nin

Remember (s/he remembers it) | Tshissitutam[u] *or* katshessitutam[u]

My friend | Nuitsheuakan

No | Mauat

Pass on (s/he passes it on to her/him) | Ashu-mineu

Read (s/he reads it) | Tshitapatam[u]

Sleep well | Tshima minukuamin

Song | Nikamun

Sovereign | Tipenimitishu

Spirit, soul | Atshak[u]

Territory | Assi *or* assit *or* nitassinan

Thank you | Tshinashkumitin

Together | Mamu

We, us, ourselves | Tshinanu

Welcome | Minu-takushini *or* Tshima minu-takushinin

Wolf | Maikan

Woman, women | Innushkueu, innushkueuat

Be wounded (s/he has a wound) | Mishkassiu

Write (s/he writes) | Mashinaitsheu

Yes | Eshe

You | Tshin

The reader interested in learning more Innu-aimun words can refer to the online *Aimun-Mashinaikan / Innu Dictionary*, http://www.innu-aimun.ca/dictionary/Words. App versions of the same dictionary also exist. Regarding Innu-aimun grammar, see the trilingual resource *Aimun-Mashinaikan / Innu Grammar / Grammaire innue* at http://grammaire.innu-aimun.ca.

APPENDIX 3

Questions for Young People

EXERCISE 1
Discussion in the classroom on the topic of racism

Objective: Introduce the issue of racism in the classroom (definition, behaviours, solutions, etc.) and discuss it in order to initiate an exchange of letters between students from two different communities.

To do this exercise, the students are asked, first of all, to form small groups in order to begin discussions. The exchange then continues with the whole class, focusing on potential solutions to fight racism.

Part A: Preparatory research

- What do you know about the history and culture of the Indigenous Peoples? Do some additional research in order to further your knowledge or reread certain passages of the book, if necessary. According to what you know now, do you agree with co-author Deni Ellis Béchard when he says on page 127 that raising the barrier of history between Indigenous and non-Indigenous people would help both communities?

- Do research on the Indian Act (1876). What does it contain? How are the Indigenous Peoples treated in it? Pay special attention to the concepts of "identity" and "territories." Are there parallels to be made with one of the demands of the Indigenous Peoples that Deni talks about on page 112?

- Certain historical figures are famous within a culture. Do research on an Indigenous leader in order to learn more about him or her. How did he or she achieved fame? For this question, reread page 129.

- Do you agree with Deni when he says, on page 13, that "Racism is built on the silence of those whom we reject and of whom we are afraid"? Do you believe, like co-author Natasha Kanapé Fontaine, that racism is "the result of knowledge and awareness not being passed on" (see page 105)? And how do you define racism? Do some research, then write a concise definition that you would give the term.

- Reread the story that Deni tells about his father on page 118. Can you, too, identify certain behaviours or attitudes of individuals that seem racist to you? Are there reactions from certain people you know personally or in society that seem to you to be racist now that you have read this book?

- Natasha, in one of her letters (on page 114), says that non-Indigenous and Indigenous communities are not so different from each other. It also has to be acknowledged that Indigenous cultures influenced non-Indigenous cultures. Very often, non-Indigenous people are not aware of the positive, historical influence that Indigenous cultures have had on their own culture. After doing some research, can you identify certain things or ways of doing things that Indigenous cultures have inspired in non-Indigenous cultures? Can you identify positive influences that Indigenous cultures have on non-Indigenous cultures today?

- Make a list of values that seem to you to be important in non-Indigenous cultures. Then make a list of values that seem to you to be important in Indigenous cultures, values that Deni calls "diverse and complex" (on page 14). Are some of these values shared? What values favour peace and sharing? Why, according to you, does Natasha place such a great importance on the value of freedom, which she mentions several times? On this topic, reread pages 75 and 76.

- Co-authors Natasha and Deni asked each other many questions about various issues in the course of their exchange of letters. For example, Deni asked Natasha, on page 88, "What is Innu culture like?" Draw up a list of questions that would permit you, too, to learn certain things about Indigenous/ non-Indigenous cultures. How could you find certain answers to those questions? What questions would you like to ask a friend your age (Indigenous or non-Indigenous)?

• Natasha talks about a passion for hockey shared by Indigenous and non-Indigenous people. Reread the anecdote about this on page 114. Which activities would you like to share with a non-Indigenous/Indigenous person? What would you tell the other person about your own culture?

Part B: Personal experiences of racism

• Deni recounts, on page 119, a situation in which he had a racist behaviour. Retell how he realized he was steeped in the racist culture in which he was living. Do you remember how you realized that racism existed? Describe that experience and explain how it influenced your life. Have you ever witnessed racist behaviour or attitudes? What did you feel?

• Natasha was confronted by prejudices about Indigenous cultures in a blog in the Québécois newspaper *Le Journal de Montréal*, as recounted by Deni on page 6. Have you ever experienced discrimination? Have you ever been the victim of prejudice? How? Have you yourself ever had prejudices against Indigenous Peoples? Which ones? Why did you think that way, say those things, or have that attitude? What were the consequences?

• On page 81, Deni talks about the concept of "invisible privilege." Reread the passage. Do you think that you have privileges that could be called "invisible"? Are there other people who have privileges that you don't have?

- Deni talks in one of his letters, on page 97, about the pejorative words used by anglophones to designate francophones: this demonstrates a form of discrimination by one culture toward another. Make a list of the discriminatory and racist terms that you know. Think of words that arouse the fear and suspicion that we sometimes feel toward people we do not know well. Now, using role playing or theatre, interpret a fictional character by putting yourself in the place of another individual talking about your culture: according to you, what could that person say? Could he or she use racist vocabulary?

Part C: How do we fight racism?
What are the solutions?

- How can we fight racism today and encourage openness to difference? Do you also believe, as Deni states on pages 126 and 127, that writing is a good way to encourage open-mindedness?

- According to you, what are the projects (social, cultural, economic, political) that could be created to bring non-Indigenous and Indigenous people together? Does this book encourage people to come together, in your view?

- Often, people feel that they are powerless to change things. Do you agree with Deni when he says, on page 134, that it is necessary, first of all, to understand the society before we can change it? Do you believe that you could fight against racism through some of your actions? Think of what you could do to raise the consciousness of your friends and family on the issue of racism and give examples.

- Deni talks about his father who was racist, who did not like Indigenous people (for example, on page 24), but Natasha also calls into question her own racism, on page 102. Think of someone you know whose behaviour or words seem racist to you. Make a list of questions that you would like to ask that person in order to better understand why he or she is racist. Do you believe that you could have a discussion with this person in order to counteract his or her racist arguments? If yes, how?

- Do you also believe that the first step toward learning to appreciate differences is to express a desire to work together and resolve the problem, as Deni suggests on page 60? If you were leader in your community, how would you go about eliminating the problem of racism? Imagine a concrete action.

EXERCISE 2
Letter exchange projects between students from different communities and cultures

Objective: Begin an exchange of letters with a person from another culture.

During the exchange, ask questions about various subjects:

- invisible privilege,
- racist heritage,
- stereotypes and prejudices,
- his or her view of history, etc.

Discuss together the fear and suspicion that can feed racism.

Examples of questions to get the exchange going:

- Where are you from?

- Tell me the history of your nation, or of your community.

- What do you know about the history of Indigenous Peoples?

- How do you see the history of colonization?

- There are more than fifty Indigenous nations in Canada. What are the differences between these nations? Are there differences between the regions of Canada?

- Have you ever experienced discrimination or prejudice? How? Have you ever felt prejudices toward Indigenous Peoples? Which ones? What changed your views?

- How many languages do you speak? Which language do you speak most often with your friends, your family? What for you is the importance of your mother tongue?

- Did you grow up in an Indigenous community? Have you ever been to an Indigenous community? If you did, how would you describe it?

- People often know little about the history of Indigenous Peoples. What do you know about their history?

- Have you ever watched APTN (Aboriginal Peoples Television Network)? If you did, what is your favourite program on that network?

EXERCISE 3
Other projects to be done as a group

Objective: This exercise consists of preparing a project to increase awareness among students about the problems caused by racism.

- Organize a lecture by an Indigenous person, an immigrant, and/or a Québécois so that he or she can share experiences in Canada and his or her views on racism.

- Reconstruct the history of Canada or of a Canadian province from the perspective of Indigenous Peoples: analyze colonialism from the perspective of the Indigenous Peoples, taking into account its consequences for their culture, their traditions, their languages, their territories, and their history.

- Reconstruct the history of cultural genocide based on the 2007 film *The Invisible Nation* by Richard Desjardins and Robert Monderie, which Natasha mentions in one of her letters (on page 30). After watching the film, give examples of things that were done to Indigenous people that were aimed at destroying their culture. Think about what is being done today. Is it very different?

- Reconstruct the events of the 1990 Oka Crisis that Natasha talks about on pages 47 and 54–57, and look for solutions that could have brought about a rapprochement between Indigenous and non-Indigenous participants in those circumstances.

- What do you think of this statement by Deni on page 98?

  I hope that the Québécois [...] can understand that the cultural oppression they inflict on Indigenous people is worse than that which they themselves have experienced. If we can succeed in seeing how much oppression has harmed our own people, perhaps it is easier to understand its effect on other groups.

- Do you believe that the cultural oppression of Indigenous people affects the Québécois today? If yes, how?

- As a group, make a list of important themes related to racism and of challenges created by this problem for a given society. Then choose a theme and write a short essay in which you analyze it. For example, you could choose the theme of dispossession, discussed by Natasha on pages 93–94, and discuss in your text the dispossession of Indigenous lands by certain private companies and by governments. Next, read the texts in the classroom. The readings can be followed by discussions focusing on the search for solutions.

ACKNOWLEDGMENTS

DENI ELLIS BÉCHARD

I would like to thank Élodie Comtois and Barbara Caretta-Debays and the team at Éditions Écosociété for their support for this book from its earliest stages. I am also grateful to Kevin Williams for his commitment to publishing it in English, as well as to Charles Simard, Howard Scott, and everyone at Talonbooks. Above all, I would like to thank Natasha for her courage, perseverance, and insight, which made this book possible in the first place.

NATASHA KANAPÉ FONTAINE

Rodney Saint-Éloi and Éditions Mémoire d'encrier, for the transmission of knowledge; Éditions Écosociété (Élodie and Barbara), for their support from the beginning. It would not have been possible without you. Deni, for this journey and for this strong and solid friendship. You are like an older brother to me.

The Innu women who stood up with me in the face of austerity. Without you there would be no value in our struggle for self-determination and a decolonized recognition.

ABOUT THE AUTHORS

DENI ELLIS BÉCHARD is the author of *Vandal Love* (Commonwealth Writers' Prize for Best First Book); *Of Bonobos and Men* (Nautilus Book Award for Investigative Journalism and Nautilus Book Award Grand Prize); *Cures for Hunger*, a memoir about his father who robbed banks (Amazon.ca Editors' Pick: Best Books of 2012); and *Into the Sun* (2016 Midwest Book Award for Fiction and selected by Radio-Canada's *Ici on lit* as one of 2017's "Incontournables," a list of the most important books of the year to be read by Canada's political leaders).

He has reported from India, Cuba, Rwanda, Colombia, Iraq, the Democratic Republic of the Congo, and Afghanistan. He has been a finalist for a National Magazine Award, has been featured in Tightrope Books' *Best Canadian Essays 2017*, and his photojournalism has been exhibited in the Canadian Museum of Human Rights. His articles, fiction, and photographs have been published in newspapers and magazines around the world, including the *Los Angeles Times*, *Salon*, *Reuters*, the *Guardian*, *Patagonia*, *La Repubblica*, the *Walrus*, *Pacific Standard*, *Le Devoir*, *Vanity Fair Italia*, the *Herald*, the *Huffington Post*, *Harvard Review*, *National Post*, and *Foreign Policy*.

PHOTO BY JULIE ARTACHO

Born in 1991, **NATASHA KANAPÉ FONTAINE** is Innu, originally from Pessamit on Quebec's North Shore. Poet-performer, actor, visual artist, and activist for Indigenous and environmental rights, she lives in Montreal. Her first collection of poems, *Do Not Enter My Soul in Your Shoes* (translated by Howard Scott; Mawenzi House, 2015), recounts her initial identity questioning and was hailed by critics, earning her the 2013 Prix littéraire des Écrivains francophones d'Amérique. A finalist at the 2015 Prix Émile-Nelligan, her second collection *Assi Manifesto* (Mawenzi House, 2016) offers a song to our planet Earth, suffocating as a result of the exploitation of natural resources, of tar sands in particular. Her third collection of poetry, *Blueberries and Apricots* (Mawenzi House, 2018) carries "the speech of the Indigenous woman, coming back to life to reverse history." Translated into English by Howard Scott, Kanapé Fontaine's books are now crossing borders and delighting audiences in Canada and around the world. She is often a guest poet, notably in Haiti, Belgium, France, Germany, Colombia, Scotland, and New Zealand (Aotearoa).

ABOUT THE TRANSLATOR

HOWARD SCOTT lives in Montreal and translates books of poetry, fiction, and non-fiction. His translation of *The Euguelion* by Louky Bersianik won the Governor General's Literary Award for French-to-English Translation in 1997. He often collaborates with Phyllis Aronoff, and in 2001 they won the Quebec Writers' Federation Literary Award for Translation. He is a past president of the Literary Translators' Association of Canada. In 2017 he was shortlisted for the Governor General's Literary Award for French-to-English Translation for Gérard Bouchard's *Social Myths and Collective Imaginaries*.